I0223989

The Gen X Series

MATHS OLYMPIAD

1

Useful for Maths Olympiads Conducted at School, National & International Levels

Author
Shraddha Singh

Peer Reviewer
Nisha Dhiman

Strictly According to the Latest Syllabus of Maths Olympiad

V&S PUBLISHERS

Published by:

V&S PUBLISHERS

F-2/16, Ansari road, Daryaganj, New Delhi-110002
☎ 23240026, 23240027 • *Fax:* 011-23240028
✉ info@vspublishers.com • 🌐 www.vspublishers.com

Online Brandstore: amazon.in/vspublishers

Regional Office : Hyderabad
5-1-707/1, Brij Bhawan (Beside Central Bank of India Lane)
Bank Street, Koti, Hyderabad - 500 095
☎ 040-24737290
✉ vspublishershyd@gmail.com

Follow us on: f t in

BUY OUR BOOKS FROM: | AMAZON | | FLIPKART |

© **Copyright:** *V&S* PUBLISHERS
ISBN 978-93-579405-0-4
New Edition

DISCLAIMER

While every attempt has been made to provide accurate and timely information in this book, neither the author nor the publisher assumes any responsibility for errors, unintended omissions or commissions detected therein. The author and publisher makes no representation or warranty with respect to the comprehensiveness or completeness of the contents provided.

All matters included have been simplified under professional guidance for general information only, without any warranty for applicability on an individual. Any mention of an organization or a website in the book, by way of citation or as a source of additional information, doesn't imply the endorsement of the content either by the author or the publisher. It is possible that websites cited may have changed or removed between the time of editing and publishing the book.

Results from using the expert opinion in this book will be totally dependent on individual circumstances and factors beyond the control of the author and the publisher.

It makes sense to elicit advice from well informed sources before implementing the ideas given in the book. The reader assumes full responsibility for the consequences arising out from reading this book.

For proper guidance, it is advisable to read the book under the watchful eyes of parents/guardian. The buyer of this book assumes all responsibility for the use of given materials and information.

The copyright of the entire content of this book rests with the author/publisher. Any infringement/transmission of the cover design, text or illustrations, in any form, by any means, by any entity will invite legal action and be responsible for consequences thereon.

Publisher's Note

General Trade and Mass Appeal books across various genres have helped **V&S Publishers** to gain widespread popularity. In a short span of 10 years, we have successfully published more than 1000 titles across 9 languages in our 50 subject categories. Being into the publishing business for about 40 years, we have always been a dynamic publishing house, with a massive distribution network, across India; including E-commerce platforms.

Understanding the need of inculcating knowledge and developing a spirit of healthy competition amongst students to make them ready for the world outside schools and colleges; we created Olympiad Series under the **GEN X SERIES Imprint** which, owning to its rich content and unique representation became popular amongst students, in no time. The motivation is not to improve marks in terms of numbers, but is to make sure that the students are already prepared to face competitive environment with respect to college admissions and cracking various entrance examinations, while ensuring their conceptual clarity.

Published for classes 1-10 across subjects English, Mathematics, Science, Computers, General Knowledge, the books are unlike any other in the market and are written in a guidebook pattern and exhaustively include examples and Multiple-Choice Questions.

Here, we present the latest Edition of **MATHS OLYMPIAD CLASS 1**.

Unique Features of the book are as follows:

☞ Authored by Subject Matter Experts' and Peer reviewed by School Principals and HOD's for the respective subjects

☞ Books based on principles of Applied Psychology and Bloom's Taxonomy

☞ Suited for Olympiad Examinations held at School level, National level & International Level irrespective of organizing body.

☞ The only Olympiad Book in India written in Guidebook Pattern with Concise Theory, images and illustrations.

☞ Exhaustively include Examples, MCQs, Subjective Questions, and HOTS with Answer Keys & Solutions.

☞ Multiple Model Papers for thorough practice also given inside the book with solutions.

☞ OMR sheets appended at the end of the book for simulating exam environment.

Besides, we are also planning to launch an App very soon for the Olympiad preparation which further testifies our constant endeavor to keep up with student demands. We have made sure to closely follow syllabus patterns of not only Olympiad conducting bodies but also education boards & organizations like CBSE and NCERT, to make sure that our books prove useful to students; helping them to boost their academic performance in schools as well.

P.S. While every care has been taken to ensure the correctness of the content, if you come across any error, howsoever minor, do not hesitate to discuss with teachers while pointing that out to us in no uncertain terms.

We wish you All the Best!

DISTINCTIVE

WHY OLYMPIADS?

Olympiads are just like competitive exams; conducted by various bodies at national and international levels. The aim is to experience a competitive examination at the school level and also to help students to discover their interest acrss subjects like English, Mathematics, Science and General Knowledge.

WHY V&S OLYMPIADS?

We at V&S Publishers aim to build an avid-reading student audience. Hence, our resolve is to follow an innovative pedagogic pattern which would help students to navigate through the book with utmost ease and comfort. Crisp theory practical examples and illustrations keep our book interactive and comprehensive.

01 LEARNING OBJECTIVES
They list the whole chapter as subtopics, helping the teachers to guide children in a step-by-step manner.

02 DID YOU KNOW
Enhance your knowledge by getting acquainted with some amazing facts across various subjects like science, Mathematics and English.

03 MULTIPLE CHOICE QUESTIONS
MCQs act as an excellent learning aid, helping you to understand and work on your mistakes.

04 THINGS TO REMEMBER
A quick recap of the chapter in a summarized format helps in faster revision along with conceptual clarity.

05 HOTS
The High Order Thinking Questions aim to help the student to solve Application-based questions and gain practical understanding of the subject.

FEATURES

SUBJECTIVE QUESTIONS

Help to place the knowledge gained in orderly fashion by using **"WH"** questions, mostly in the form of bullet points.

06

ACHIEVER'S SECTION

Offers a quick revision of the book along with some new facts for the students to discover.

07

A SET OF OMR SHEETS

To allow the student to practice question in an exam-like format which would help them to get the "feel" of how Olympiad exams take place.

08

MODEL TEST PAPERS

Two model test papers are provided at the end of each book, which help the student to test the knowledge which they have gained after thorough reading of all chapters.

09

ANSWER KEY & SOLUTIONS

Detailed Answer Key along with explanations aid the pupil to indentify, understand the mistakes they make during the course of Olympiad preparation.

10

COMPLEMENT SCHOOL SYLLABI

The syllabi across all Olympiad examination closely follow the pattern of academic books. Hence, they not only provide a competitive examination experience, but also help to revise topics for school examinations as well, while strengthening conceptual precision.

ENHANCEMENT OF ANALYTICAL & LOGICAL REASONING

Practicing analytical ability questions, not only helps in developing intellectual ability but also plays a vital role in building critical thinking ability which helps an individual to think about a question or a crisis like situation in day to day life; from all aspects and directions.

Note to Parents

Dear Parents,

Olympiad examinations come with a plethora of advantages. First and foremost among such advantages is the application of knowledge studied, in the form of multiple-choice questions. It helps the child not only to step away from rote learning, but also helps them to exhibit their competencies across various subjects.

In addition to this, Olympiads help the student to understand the importance of revision and practice, and to imbibe upon these practices; which also prove useful in academic performance of the child.

The Olympiads are conducted across multiple subjects, and help the child to recognize their field of interest, thereby encouraging the students to make a career in the field where they can excel the most.

However, cognitive development of a child is not just limited to the four walls of classroom. Following steps can be encouraged by you, to ensure their ward is able to grasp various concepts with ease or lesser difficulty:

☞ **Eat a balanced diet:** Ensure intake of vitamins and minerals to keep you active. Include fruits and super foods like millet in your diet to ensure healthy functioning of organs. Huge intake of junk food should be avoided.

☞ **Indulge in outdoor activities:** Outdoor games break the monotony of life. Play your heart out in greenery to keep yourself alert, active and fit.

☞ **Sleep well:** A sound sleep of 7-8 hours refreshes the brain and makes it ready to understand new topics with more clarity. A sleep derived person faces difficulty in doing even the simplest tasks of day to day life.

☞ **Reduce your Screen time:** More screen time leads to not only weakening of eyesight but decreases concentration span. Regulated Screen time should be encouraged

☞ **Do not hesitate to raise a hand:** Having a doubt in class? Do not hesitate to ask your parents or teachers. This ensures more Conceptual Clarity and hence leads to Application based understanding of various subjects and topics.

☞ **Teach and Learn:** No need to do rote-learning. Once you understand a topic teach or explain it to your friends, siblings and parents. It brings clarity and ensures the child does his revision this way.

☞ **Keep smiling:** A positive attitude promotes a growth mindset and encourages the child to be more inquisitive and try to learn something new, everyday!

HAPPY LEARNING!

Contents

SECTION 1
MATHEMATICAL
REASONING

Numbers

Learning Objectives : In this unit, we will learn about:
- ✓ Numerals and Counting Numbers
- ✓ Formation of Greatest and Smallest Numbers
- ✓ Number Sense (Two-Digit Numbers)
- ✓ Number Names (Numbers upto 100)
- ✓ Ordinal Numbers

CHAPTER SUMMARY

Numerals

The digits 0, 1, 2, 3, 4, 5, 6, 7, 8 and 9 are used to form numbers or numerals.

1 2 3 4 5 6 7 8 9 0

Counting Numbers

The numbers 1, 2, 3.... used to count things are called **counting numbers**.

One, two, three.......are called **number names** of 1, 2, 3....

1	ONE
2	TWO
3	THREE
4	FOUR
5	FIVE
6	SIX
7	SEVEN
8	EIGHT
9	NINE

Ones and Tens

☐ + ☐☐☐ ☐☐☐ ☐☐☐ makes ☐☐☐ ☐☐☐ ☐☐☐ ☐ equals 1 ten

1 one and 9 ones

10 ones

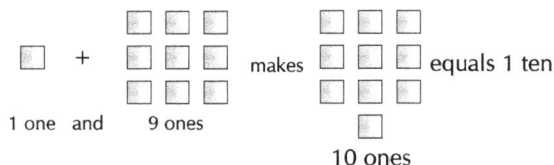

Note : 0 does not have any value on its own, but acts as a place holder.

Formation of Greatest and Smallest Numbers

Greatest Numbers

For forming the greatest 2-digit numbers, place the bigger digit at tens place and the smaller digits at ones place.

Example: Form greatest number using digits 7 and 9.

Solution: Greatest number = 97

Smallest Numbers

For forming the smallest 2-digit numbers, place the smaller digit at tens and the bigger digit at ones place.

Example : Form smallest number using digits 5 and 7.

Solution: Smallest number = 57

TRIVIA

1000 is the only number from 0 to 1000 that has "a" in it.

Ordinal Numbers

Numbers such as 1st, 2nd, 3rd, 4th, 5th, 6th, 7th, 8th, 9th, and 10th specify the position of an object in an ordered collection. These numbers are called **positional numbers** or **ordinal numbers**.

First, Second, Third…. are the ordinal numbers for 1, 2, 3….

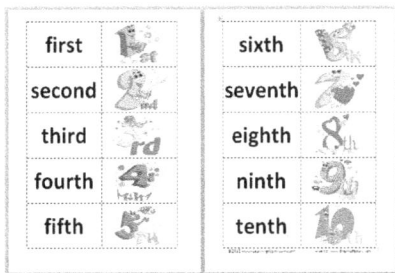

Number Sense (Two-Digit Numbers)

A two-digit number can be written in tens and ones.

For example, 25 = 2 tens and 5 ones

Numbers upto 20 :

11	12	13	14	15
Eleven	Twelve	Thirteen	Fourteen	Fifteen

16	17	18	19	20
Sixteen	Seventeen	Eighteen	Nineteen	Twenty

Number Names (Numbers upto 100)

Number	Number Name	Number of ten
10	Ten	1
20	Twenty	2
30	Thirty	3
40	Forty	4
50	Fifty	5
60	Sixty	6
70	Seventy	7
80	Eighty	8
90	Ninety	9

Important Points

➤ A one-digit number is smaller than a two-digit number.

➤ Smallest two-digit number is 1 more than largest one-digit number i.e. 10 is 1 more than 9.

➤ 10 is the smallest two-digit number and 99 is the largest two-digit number.

➤ Smallest three-digit number is 1 more than the largest two-digit number i.e. 100 is 1 more than 99.

➤ 100 is the smallest three-digit number.

➤ Every number (except 0) is 1 more than its previous number and 1 less than its next number.

➤ All one-digit numbers have only the ones place.

➤ 1 is the smallest and 9 is the greatest one-digit counting numbers.

➤ Two-digit numbers have two places – The ones place and the tens place. 10 is the smallest two-digit counting number, written using the digits 0 and 1.

➡ The digits 0, 1, 2, 3, 4, 5, 6, 7, 8 and 9 are used to form numbers or numerals.

➡ 0 does not have any value on its own, but acts as a place holder.

➡ Every number (except 0) is 1 more than its previous number and 1 less than its next number.

1. Which of the following has 6 objects?

(a)

(b)

(c)

(d)

2. Which of the following has three objects?

(a)

(b)

(c)

(d)

3. The greatest one- digit number is 9. What is its number name?

   (a) Ten   (b) Nine

   (c) Five   (d) Two

4. Which of the following is correct?

   (a) 7–Six   (b) 6–Three

   (c) 5–Five   (d) 9–Eight

5. Choose the one that is wrong.

   (a) Four – 4   (b) Seven – 7

   (c) Nine – 9   (d) One – 0

6. Which of the following is correct?

(a)		7
(b)		5
(c)		3
(d)		8

7. Choose the correct number of objects for "Four".

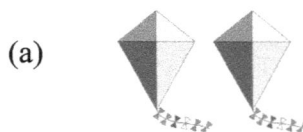

(a)

(b)

(c)

(d)

(b)

(c)

(d)

8. Which of the following is matched correctly?

(a)		2
(b)		8
(c)		9
(d)		3

9. Match the number of objects to their number names.

	Column I		Column II
(A)		(i)	Seven
(B)		(ii)	Three
(C)		(iii)	Four
(D)		(iv)	Five

(a) A - i, B - ii, C - iii, D - iv
(b) A - iv, B - ii, C - i, D - iii
(c) A - ii, B - iv, C - i, D - iii
(d) A - iii, B - ii, C - i, D - iv

10. Select the group with 8 objects.

(a)

11. Match the numbers to the objects.

	Column I		Column II
(A)	5	(i)	
(B)	2	(ii)	
(C)	8	(iii)	
(D)	9	(iv)	

(a) A - i, B - iv, C - ii, D - iii
(b) A - iii, B - iv, C - i, D - ii
(c) A - ii, B - iii, C - iv, D - i
(d) A - iii, B - ii, C - iv, D - i

12. Choose the number name for the number of objects in the box

(a) Nine   (b) Seven

(c) Six   (d) Eight

13. Choose the correct number of objects for 'Ten'.

(a)

(b)

(c)

(d)

14. What is the ordinal number of 7?

(a) First   (b) Seventh

(c) Sixth   (d) Ninth

15. Which number comes after 28?

(a) Twenty nine   (b) Twenty six

(c) Twenty seven   (d) Twenty three

16. Which of the following is 1 more than 4?

(a)

(b)

(c)

(d)

17. Choose the correct number of the given objects.

(a) 8   (b) 10

(c) 9   (d) 7

18. Which object is at fourth position in the set given?

(a) Ball   (b) Chair

(c) Key   (d) Book

19. Who is standing in the third place in the line?

(a) Ashu   (b) Navneet

(c) Shraddha   (d) Ashima

20. Which bowl has minimum number of apples

(i)   (ii)   (iii)   (iv)

(a) (i)   (b) (ii)

(c) (iii)   (d) (iv)

1. What is the number name of the smallest two-digit number?
   (a) One   (b) Zero
   (c) Ten   (d) Nine

2. Which of the following has numbers in an order?

(a)	4	2	0	6
(b)	3	5	7	10
(c)	7	9	2	3
(d)	6	7	8	5

3. Which of the following has objects 1 less than 8?
   (a)
   (b)
   (c)
   (d)

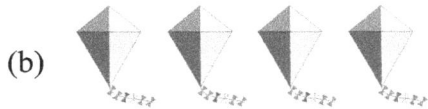

4. Match the objects that are same in numbers.

Column I	Column II
(a)	(i)
(b)	(ii)

| (c) | (iii) |
| (d) | (iv) |

5. Choose the correct subtraction sentence for the given picture.

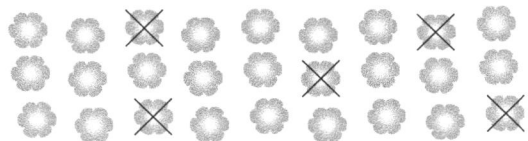

   (a) 2 tens 3 ones – 4 ones
   (b) 2 tens 4 ones – 5 ones
   (c) 2 tens 7 ones – 5 ones
   (d) 2 tens 4 ones – 4 ones

1. Arrange the following numbers in ascending order:

   3, 9, 7, 16, 15

   Answer:

   The correct answer is 3, 7, 9, 15, 16.

   To solve this first we write smallest number that is 3. Then again write the smallest number from the remaining numbers that is 7 and thus continue in the same way. The numbers are arranged in the ascending order.

2. What number comes between 3 and 5?

   Answer:

   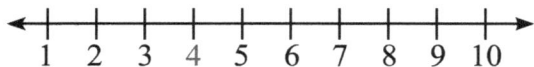

   4 comes between 3 and 5

3. Put the correct symbol > or < in the blank space.

   6 ____ 8

   Answer:

   On the number line, '6' lies to the left of '8'.

   So, 6 is less than 8

   Hence, 6<8

4. Subtract 57 from 98

   Answer:

   Step1: Place the number one below the other.

   ```
      T  O
      9  8
   -  5  7
   _____
   ```

   Step 2: Subtract the ones

   ```
      T  O
      9  8
   -  5  7
   _____
         1
   ```

   8 ones – 7 ones = 1 one

   Step 3: Subtract the tens

   ```
      T  O
      9  8
   -  5  7
   _____
      4  1
   ```

   9 tens – 5 tens = 4 tens

5. Add 35 and 18

   Answer:

   Step 1: Place the number one below the other.

   ```
      T  O
      3  5
   +  1  8
   _____
   ```

   Step 2: Add the ones

   ```
   1  T  O
      3  5
   +  1  8
   _____
         3
   ```

   5 ones and 8 ones make 13 ones = 1 ten and 3 ones

   3 is written in the ones column of the answer and 1 is carried over to the tens column

   Step 3: Add the tens

   ```
   1  T  O
      3  5
   +  1  8
   _____
      5  3
   ```

   3 tens + 1 ten + 1 ten (carried over) = 5 tens

   5 is written in the tens column of the answer

Addition

2

Learning Objectives : In this unit, we will learn about:
- ✓ Properties of Addition
- ✓ Addition of Two-Digit Numbers (without regrouping)
- ✓ Addition of Two-Digit Numbers (with regrouping)

CHAPTER SUMMARY

Addition

Counting things together is called **addition**. The words total, sum, add, more, in all, altogether, etc., mean addition.

The symbol for addition is '**+**' and it is read as plus.

Addend

The numbers that are added are called addends and the answer we get on adding is called **sum**.

$$8 + 3 = 11$$

Addend   Addend   Sum

A line with numbers at equal places on it is called a **number line**. Addition is shown using number line.

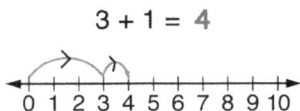

$$3 + 1 = 4$$

0 1 2 3 4 5 6 7 8 9 10

Properties of Addition

(i) Adding 0 to number gives the same number as the sum. For example : $5 + 0 = 5$.

$0 + 1 = 1$	$0 + 6 = 6$	$0 + 11 = 11$
$0 + 2 = 2$	$0 + 7 = 7$	$0 + 12 = 12$
$0 + 3 = 3$	$0 + 8 = 8$	$0 + 13 = 13$
$0 + 4 = 4$	$0 + 9 = 9$	$0 + 14 = 14$
$0 + 5 = 5$	$0 + 10 = 10$	$0 + 15 = 15$

$0 + 16 = 16$	$0 + 21 = 21$
$0 + 17 = 17$	$0 + 22 = 22$
$0 + 18 = 18$	$0 + 23 = 23$
$0 + 19 = 19$	$0 + 24 = 24$
$0 + 20 = 20$	$0 + 25 = 25$

(ii) **Order of Numbers :** If we change the order of numbers the sum remains the same (i.e. $3 + 4 = 4 + 3$)

$$3 + 4 = 4$$
$$+ 3 = 7$$

Addition of Two-Digit Numbers (without regrouping)

Example : Add 43 and 5.

Solution :

Step 1 : Write the number in the tens and ones column.

```
  T   O
  4   3
+     5
-------
      8
```

Step 2: Add the digits of ones column

```
    T   O
    4   3
+       5
_____
        8
```

Step 3: Add the digits of tens column.

```
    T   O
    4   3
+       5
_____
    4   8
```

TRIVIA

40 when written "forty" is the only number with letters in alphabetical order, while "one" is the only one with letters in reverse order

Addition of Two Digit Numbers (with regrouping)

When the sum of ones digits exceeds 10, we regroup the sum into tens and ones.

Example : Add 27 and 8.

Solution :

Step 1 : Add the digits of ones column

7 ones + 8 ones = 15 ones

Regroup 15 ones.

15 ones = 1 ten + 5 ones

Write 1 is tens place above the number.

Step 2: Add the digits of tens column.

1 tens (regrouped) + 2 tens = 3 tens

Write 3 is the tens place.

27 + 8 = 35

MUST REMEMBER

➡ Counting things together is called addition. The words total, sum, add, more, in all, altogether, etc., mean addition.

➡ A line with numbers at equal places on it is called a number line.

1. Choose the correct addition fact for the given figure

   and

   is

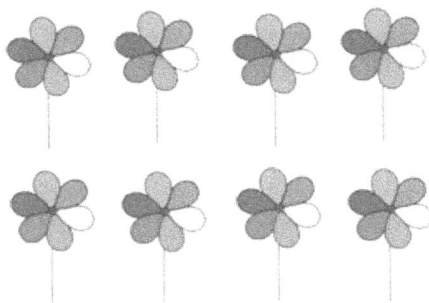

   (a) $4 + 4 = 8$ (b) $4 + 3 = 7$
   (c) $3 + 4 = 8$ (d) $3 + 3 = 8$

2. Look at the given figure.

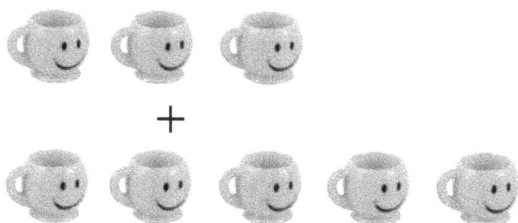

   $3 + 5 = ?$

   Find the number which comes in place of the question mark.
   (a) 9   (b) 8
   (c) 10   (d) 7

3. The adding machine adds 4 to any number that is put in it and sends the sum out. What is the sum when 5 is put into the machine?
   (a) 6   (b) 8
   (c) 3   (d) 9

4. Which of the following is incorrect sum?
   (a) $6 + 3 = 9$ (b) $6 + 4 = 11$
   (c) $5 + 4 = 9$ (d) $4 + 4 = 8$

5. Look at the figure below :

   Which number must be placed in place of '*'.
   (a) 0   (b) 3
   (c) 2   (d) 6

6. There are 7 apples in a basket. 2 more apples are put in it. How many apples are there in the basket?
   (a) 9   (b) 5
   (c) 7   (d) 0

Question 7 to 10 : Look at the figure given :

Class 1A		Class 1B		Class 1C	
21	23	24	20	21	20

7. How many students in all are there in class 1A?
   (a) 41   (b) 43
   (c) 42   (d) 44

8. How many girls are in class 1A, 1B and 1C altogether?
   (a) 40   (b) 63
   (c) 43   (d) 36

9. How many boys are in classes 1A and 1C?
   (a) 42   (b) 44
   (c) 41   (d) 40

10. Which two classes have the same number of girls?
    (a) 1A and 1C   (b) 1A and 1B
    (c) 1B and 1C   (d) Either A or B

11. Which of the following is correct sum?
    (a) $3 + 4 = 9$ (b) $5 + 5 = 10$
    (c) $2 + 6 = 9$ (d) $1 + 5 = 8$

12. Which is more?

(a) $50 + 6$ (b) $50 + 9$

(c) $60 + 12$ (d) $50 + 3$

13.

20 Flowers   54 Flowers   +   = ... flowers,

(a) 80   (b) 74
(c) 82   (d) 79

14. I have 5 chocolates. Sonu gave me 4 more. Ravi gave me 3 more. How many sweets I have?
    (a) $3 + 4 + 2 = 9$ (b) $5 + 4 + 3 = 12$
    (c) $3 + 2 + 6 = 11$ (d) $3 + 4 + 6 = 13$

15. Number of flower in both boxes
    = _____

     Box A   **Box B**

   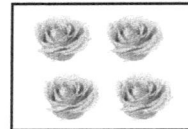

(a) $8 + 5 = 13$ (b) $6 + 4 = 10$
(c) $8 + 6 = 14$ (d) $8 + 4 = 12$

16. Shraddha and Shubhra are playing a card game.

Shraddha

Shubhra

What is the sum of the numbers of Shubhra's cards?
(a) 8   (b) 5
(c) 3   (d) 10

17. Golu collected 35 stamps and Ankit collected 43 stamps.

Golu   Ankit

How many stamps will the boys have in all?
(a) 75   (b) 78
(c) 87   (d) 68

18. Shraddha got 38 marks in science and 50 marks in maths.

    Science   Maths
    38   50

    How many marks did she get in all?
    (a) 68   (b) 58
    (c) 88   (d) 80

19. Radha's mother bought 10 apples on Monday, 14 apples on Wednesday and 25 apples on Sunday. How many apples did her mother buy altogether?
    (a) 47   (b) 40
    (c) 49   (d) 48

20. Priya has 6 dolls.

    Pooja has 3 dolls.

    Total number of dolls = …………
    (a) 12   (b) 11
    (c) 10   (d) 9

HOTS

1. What comes in between?

    31 + 2   ?   32 + 3

    (a) 31 + 4   (b) 30 + 4
    (c) 32 + 4   (d) 33 − 4

2. Add the balloons given below and choose the correct option.

    (a)   (b)

    (c)   (d)

3.

(a)   (b)

(c)   (d)

4. There are 4 legs in a chair. In a room there are 3 chairs. How many legs do these three chairs have?
   (a) 7 legs   (b) 11 legs
   (c) 12 legs   (d) none of these

5. In a garden there are 4 plants of Marigold, 3 plants of Jasmine and 7 plants of roses. How many plants are there in all in the garden?
   (a) 14 plants   (b) 12 plants
   (c) 16 plants   (d) 18 plants

1. How many bananas are there in all?

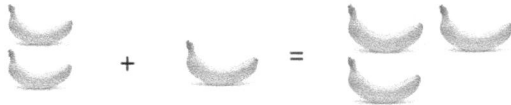

Answer: 2 bananas and 1 banana is equal to 3 bananas

Hence $2 + 1 = 3$

2. Add 3 and 3

Answer:

Step 1: Place one number above the other.

	3	
+	3	

Step 2: Draw vertical bars for each number.

	3				
+	3			

Step 3: Count all vertical bars and write the answer in the box.

	3				
+	3				
	6							

3. There are three balls in box A

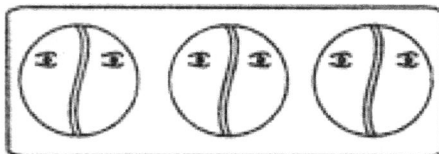

Three balls

There is one ball in another box B

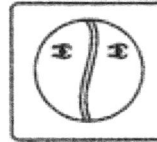

One ball

Now,

How many balls are there in both the boxes together?

Answer: For this, we put the balls from both the boxes in a single box as shown below:

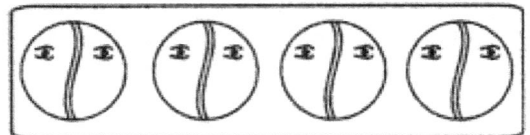

Four balls

Therefore, the third box has three balls of box A and one ball of box B and they are together 4 balls.

Let's understand it in another way:

Three balls   **One ball**

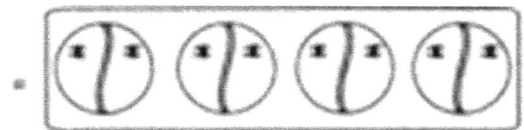

Four balls

or

$3 + 1 = 4$

Where '+' is sign of addition and it is read as 'plus' and '=' is the sign of 'is equal to' or 'is same as'

4. Add the numbers inside the egg given below.

Answer:

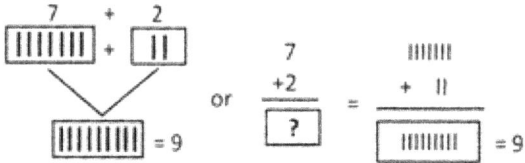

5. Study the given sets and answer the following questions.

Find the total number of flowers in set Q and set R.

Answer:

Number of flowers in set Q = 12

Number of flowers in set R = 23

Total number of flowers in set Q and set R = 12 + 23 = 35

Subtraction

Learning Objectives : In this unit, we will learn about:
- ✓ Properties of Subtraction
- ✓ Subtraction of Two - Digit Numbers (without regrouping)
- ✓ Subtraction of Two - Digit Numbers (with regrouping)

CHAPTER SUMMARY

Subtraction

Taking away some items from a group is called **subtraction**.

➤ Subtraction is the opposite of addition.

➤ The words difference, left, remaining, taken away, less 'etc'. mean subtraction.

➤ The symbol for subtraction is '−'. It is read as minus.

Minuend : The number from which another number is taken away is called **minuend.**

Subtrahend : The number that is taken away is called **subtrahend.**

Difference : The answer we get by subtracting a given number from other is called **difference**.

$$8 - 3 = 5$$

Minuend   Subtrahend   Difference

We can subtract numbers using a number line. For example : $7 - 4 = 3$

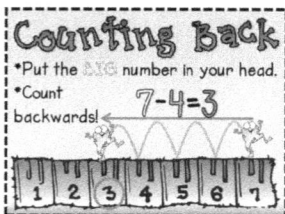

Properties of Subtraction

(i) Subtracting 0 from a number gives the number itself as difference.

For example : $5 - 0 = 5$

(ii) Subtracting a number from the number itself gives 0 as difference.

For example: $5 - 5 = 0$

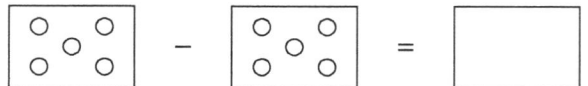

Subtraction of Two-Digit Numbers (without regrouping)

Example : Subtract 5 from 39.

Solution : **Step 1:** Writing the number in ones and tens columns as shown.

```
    T   O
    3   9
 −      5
 ─────────
```

Step 2: Subtracting ones digits.

$$
\begin{array}{cc}
\text{T} & \text{O} \\
3 & 9 \\
- & 5 \\
\hline
 & 4 \\
\end{array}
$$

Step 3: Subtracting tens digits.

$$
\begin{array}{cc}
\text{T} & \text{O} \\
3 & 9 \\
- & 5 \\
\hline
3 & 4 \\
\end{array}
$$

TRIVIA

"FOUR" is the only number in the English language that is spelt with the same number of letters as the number itself

Subtraction of Two-Digit Numbers (with regrouping)

Example : Subtract 9 from 55.

Solution: Step 1: Subtract digit at ones column.

Since 5 is less than 9, 9 cannot be subtracted from 5. So we borrow 1 ten from 5 tens. Now, we have 4 at tens place and 15 at ones place.

$$
\begin{array}{cc}
\text{T} & \text{O} \\
4 & 15 \\
5 & 5 \\
- & 9 \\
\hline
4 & 6 \\
\end{array}
$$

5 tens – 1 ten = 4 tens remain in the tens column. In the ones column, we have
1 ten + 5 ones = 10 ones + 5 ones = 15 ones

Now subtract 9 ones from 14 ones.

15 ones – 9 ones = 6 ones

Write 6 in the ones column. Subtract 4 tens from zero

4 tens – 0 = 4 tens.

Thus, 55 – 9 = 46

Subtraction through Addition
We can check subtraction by adding the difference between two numbers to the smallest number. If we get the bigger number as the sum the subtraction is correct, otherwise it is incorrect.

MUST REMEMBER

➡ The words difference, left, remaining, taken away, less 'etc'. mean subtraction.
➡ Subtracting 0 from a number gives the number itself as difference.
➡ Subtracting a number from the number itself gives 0 as difference.
➡ We can check subtraction by adding the difference between two numbers to the smallest number. If we get the bigger number as the sum the subtraction is correct, otherwise it is incorrect.

1. What is 4 tens 3 ones minus 2 tens 2 ones?
   - (a) 21
   - (b) 12
   - (c) 23
   - (d) 23

2. Golu had

   He gave  to his brother.

   How many are left with him?

   - (a)
   - (b)
   - (c)
   - (d)

3. How is 12 less than 30 written?
   - (a) $30 - 12 = 18$
   - (b) $30 - 18 = 12$
   - (c) $18 - 12 = 6$
   - (d) $30 - 6 = 24$

4. Which is same as $13 - 3$?
   - (a) $11 - 5$
   - (b) $15 - 5$
   - (c) $12 - 4$
   - (d) $9 - 3$

5. In Class I, there are 89 students. 42 of them are girls. How many boys are there in class I?
   - (a) 82
   - (b) 42
   - (c) 67
   - (d) 47

6. 68 oranges were in a basket. 44 were put in a bag.

   How many oranges are left in the basket?
   - (a) 84
   - (b) 24
   - (c) 48
   - (d) 42

7. 2 tens 5 ones − 1 ten 2 ones = ?
   - (a) 12
   - (b) 14
   - (c) 13
   - (d) 15

8. $\boxed{} = 20$ and $\square = 10$, then which of the

following is correct?

(a) $\boxed{} - \square = \square$

(b) $\boxed{} - \square = \square\square$

(c) $\boxed{} - \square = \boxed{}$

(d) $\boxed{} - \square = \square\boxed{}$

9. $-$ $=$

(a) 5   (b) 4
(c) 3   (d) 2

10. The difference between the greatest and the smallest number shown in the figure is _____.
    (a) 64
    (b) 82
    (c) 81
    (d) 28

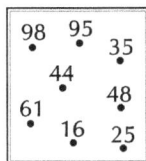

    98 95
          35
      44
         48
    61
      16 25

11. Which of the following is the another way of 7 less than 10?
    (a) $10 - 7 = 3$ (b) $7 - 5 = 2$
    (c) $12 - 5 = 7$ (d) $12 + 5 = 17$

12. $\boxed{40} - \boxed{30} = ?$
    (a) 15   (b) 10
    (c) 11   (d) 6

13.

    How many balloons are left?
    (a) 3   (b) 4
    (c) 5   (d) 7

14. There are in a pond jumped off. How many are left?
    (a) $7 - 2 = 4$ (b) $8 - 2 = 6$
    (c) $7 - 2 = 3$ (d) $7 - 2 = 1$

15. Which subtraction sentence gives same value as $8 - 2$?
    (a) $12 - 2$
    (b) $12 - 6$
    (c) $12 - 4$
    (d) $15 - 5$

16. Divesh had 69 marbles. He gave 35 marbles to Kiran. How many marbles are left with Divesh?
    (a) 34   (b) 45
    (c) 49   (d) 36

17. A book has 55 pages. Nonu reads 40 pages. How many pages are left to be read?

(a) 20　　　　　　(b) 15
(c) 25　　　　　　(d) 45

18. Shraddha has 99 sweets. She gave away 46 of them to her sister Shubhra. How many sweets does Shraddha have?
(a) 53　　　　　　(b) 43
(c) 63　　　　　　(d) 56

19. A shopkeeper sold 25 bags on Monday. He sold 5 bags less on Tuesday. How many bags are sold on Tuesday?
(a) $18 - 2 = 16$　　(b) $25 - 5 = 20$
(c) $18 + 3 = 21$　　(d) $18 - 16 = 2$

20. Manali baked 20 cakes. She gave 3 cakes to Mahima. How many cakes are left with her?
(a) 12　　　　　　(b) 15
(c) 17　　　　　　(d) 16

HOTS

1. Which of the following shows the least value?

(a) 11 ones + 5 tens　　(b) 20 ones − 6 ones

(c) 14 ones + 18 ones　　(d) 9 tens − 10 ones

2. Garima jumps 2 steps from 0, then 3 steps and then 1 step. Where will she reach ?

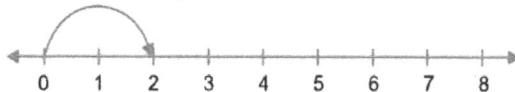

(a) 6th step　　　　(b) 7th step
(c) 8th step　　　　(d) 5th step

3. Tanuj drinks a few glasses of juice. There are___glasses of juice left. Tanuj drinks_____glasses of juice.

(a) 4, 3　　　　　　(b) 7, 5
(c) 7, 4　　　　　　(d) 3, 8

4. How many more balloons do we need to add to the given set in order to have 20 balloons in total?

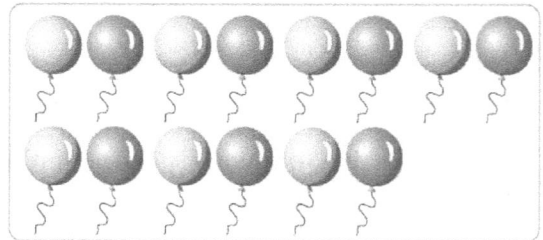

(a) 14　　　　　　(b) 6
(c) 13　　　　　　(d) 7

5. Which number comes in the place of R?

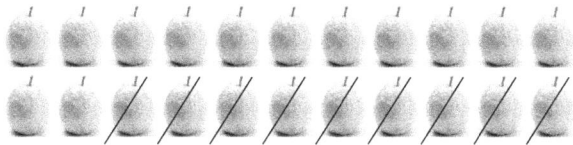

$$R - 9 = 13$$

(a) 20 (b) 22

(c) 21 (d) 24

6. How many balls should be crossed '×' to show 4 balls uncrossed?

(a) 10 (b) 6

(c) 4 (d) 2

7. Shailley has 50 chocolates. She gave 15 chocolates to Ajay and 15 chocolates to Vansh. How many chocolates are left with her?

(a) 50 (b) 30

(c) 60 (d) 20

8.  Blue buttons

Red buttons

How many more red buttons are needed so that red buttons are equal to blue buttons?

(a) 4 (b) 3

(c) 7 (d) 8

9. Which of the following number sentences represents the given picture?

(a) 22–9 = 15 (b) 22–9 = 13

(c) 20–9 = 11 (d) 20–9 = 13

10. How many ice-creams should be crossed 'X*' to show 8 ice-creams uncrossed?

(a) 14 (b) 6

(c) 4 (d) 8

SUBJECTIVE QUESTIONS

1. There were 44 books on the shelf. Tia took out 10 books to read. How many books are left on the shelf?

   Answer:

T	O
4	4
– 1	0
3	4

2. Asha bought 6 eggs. One of them is broken. How many eggs are left?

   Answer:

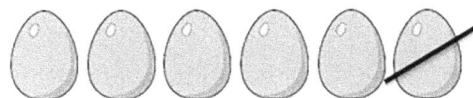

$$\begin{array}{r} 6 \\ - 1 \\ \hline 5 \end{array}$$

3. Subtract 7 – 3

   Answer:

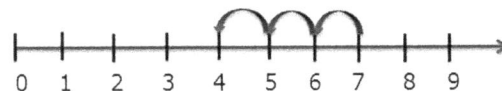

Here, 3 is subtracted from the given number i.e. 7, so we will make 3 jumps to the left of 7.

i.e. 1st jump – from 7 to 6,

2nd jump – 6 to 5

And 3rd jump – 5 to 4

Therefore, the difference of 7 and 3 is 4.

4. Subtract 18 from 57

Answer:

Step1: Place the number one below the other.

```
    T   O
    5   7
 –  1   8
 _____
```

Step 2: Subtract the ones

```
    T       O
 4  5   17  7
 –  1       8
 _____
            9
```

As 7 is smaller than 8, we cannot subtract 8 from 7. So, 1 ten is borrowed from the tens column.

Now, 1 ten = 10 ones, which means 10 ones + 7 ones = 17 ones.

We have 17 ones and we can subtract 8 ones from 17 ones.

17 ones – 8 ones = 9 ones

9 is written in the ones column of the answer

Step 3: Subtract the tens

```
    T       O
 4  5   17  7
 –  1       8
 _____
    3       9
```

After borrowing 1 ten from tens column, we have 4 tens (5 -1=4 tens) in the tens column.

Now subtract the tens

4 tens – 1 ten = 3 tens

3 is written in the tens column of the answer

5. There are 47 children in a class. 18 were absent on Monday. How many children were present on Monday?

Answer:

```
    T       O
 3  4   17  7
 –  1       8
 _____
    2       9
```

⏰⏰⏰

Measurement

Learning Objectives : In this unit, we will learn about:
- ✓ Length
- ✓ Weight
- ✓ Capacity

CHAPTER SUMMARY

Things are measured to find out how big or how heavy they are.

Length

The distance between two points is called **length**.

Words used for length:

Height : Length measured upwards.

Distance : Length measured between objects on same level.

Width : Length measured from side to side.

Depth : Length measured downwards.

Non-standard Units of Measuring Length

We can use handspans, footspans, cubits and paces to measure different lengths.

Handspan

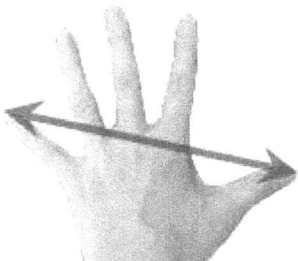

The distance from the tip of the thumb to the tip of the little finger on our outstretched hand.

Pace

Measure from the heel on one foot to the toe on our other foot.

Cubit

Measurement from back of elbow to extended finger.

We can also use other objects such as pens, pencils, paperclips to measure different lengths.

Standard Units of Measuring Length

The length of objects in terms of non-standard units differs from person to person. To avoid these differences, we use units such as metre and centimetre for accurate measurement of length.

Length

Length of an object can be measured by comparing it with the length of a known object or a ruler.

Metre rod   Ruler

Metre

It is used to measure the length of a piece of cloth. The height of a door as well as the height of a room, etc.

Metre is written as m in short.

Centimetre

It is used to measure the length of small objects like, chalk, eraser, knife, paperclip, etc.

Centimetre is written as cm in short.

1 metre = 100 centimetres or 1 m = 100 cm

Weight

Different objects have different weights.

(i)   Heaviness of an object is called **mass**, which is usually called **weight**.

(ii) Weight of an object can be measured by comparing with the weight of a known object.

Standard Units of Measuring Weight

To know the accurate weight, we use units such as kilogram and gram. Kilogram is written as kg and gram is written as gm in short.

1 kilogram = 1000 grams

TRIVIA

Have you ever noticed that the opposite sides a die always add up to seven (7).

Capacity

(i)   The amount of space inside an object is called capacity.

(ii) Capacity of an object can be measured by comparing it with the capacity of a known object or a measuring jar.

(iii) We use standard units such as litre and millilitre to measure capacity. Litre is written as *L* and millilitre is written as mL.

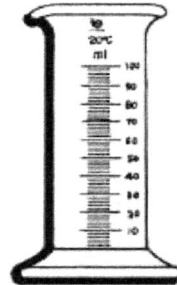

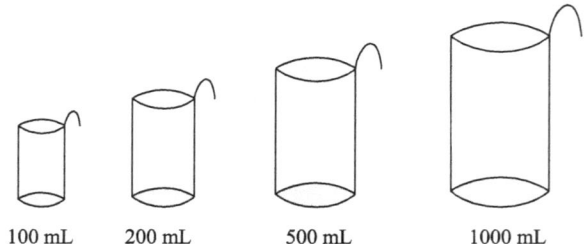

100 mL   200 mL   500 mL   1000 mL

MUST REMEMBER

➡ The length of objects in terms of non-standard units differs from person to person.
➡ Is used to measure the length of a piece of cloth.

MULTIPLE CHOICE QUESTIONS

1. Which of the following is shortest length?
   (a) 15 cm   (b) 30 cm
   (c) 28 cm   (d) 32 cm

2. Which square is the biggest?
   (a) □

   (b) ▢

   (c) ▢

   (d) ▢

3. Which of the following is smallest circle?
   (a) ○
   (b) ○
   (c) ○
   (d) ○

4. Which kite has the shortest tail??

   (a)   (b)

   (c)   (d)

5. Which of the following is the lightest?

   (a)

   (b)

   (c)

   (d)

6. Which of these is lighter than 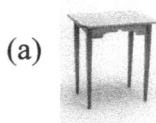 ?

   (a)    (b)

   (c)    (d)

7. Which of the two glasses have same height?
   (a) Q and S   (b) P and R
   (c) P and Q   (d) R and S

8. Spider _____ is the farthest to the top of the ladder.
   (a) P   (b) Q
   (c) R   (d) S

   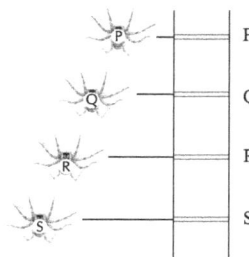

9. Which of the following picture shows the ball 1 is equal to ball 2?

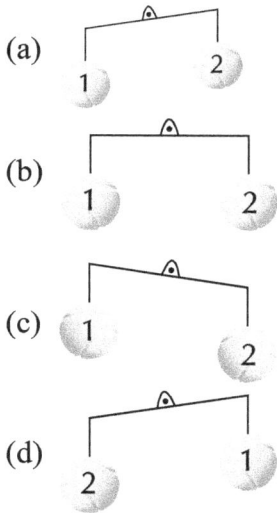

(a)

1   2

(b)

1   2

(c) 1

2

(d)

2   1

10. Which object is thinner than pencil?.

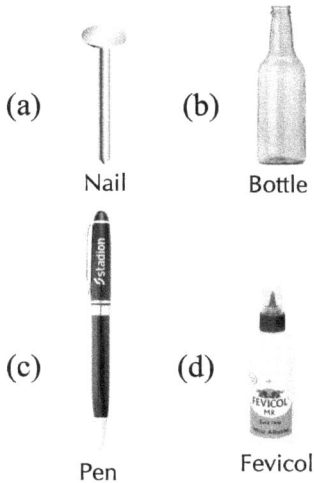

(a)

Nail

(b)

Bottle

(c)

Pen

(d)

Fevicol

Direction (11–12) : Look at different strings.

L
M
N
O

11. Which string is the longest?
    (a) L   (b) M
    (c) N   (d) O

12. Which string is the shortest?
    (a) L   (b) M
    (c) N   (d) O

13. Which penguin is nearest to the finish line?

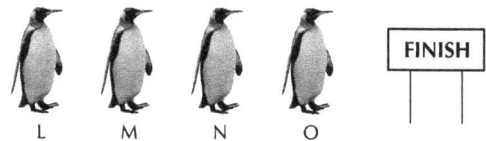

L   M   N   O   FINISH

    (a) L   (b) M
    (c) N   (d) O

14. Tape is _____ span long.

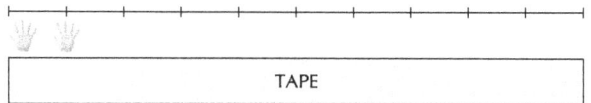

TAPE

    (a) 20   (b) 12
    (c) 13   (d) 14

15. The girl is how many units tall?

☐ = 2 units

    (a) 12 units   (b) 10 units
    (c) 14 units   (d) 16 units

16. Which tree is taller than the one given below?

(a)

(b)

(c)

(d)

17. Which of the following has the least capacity?

(a)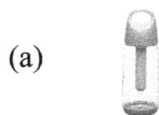

(b)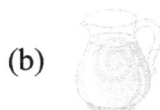

(c)

(d)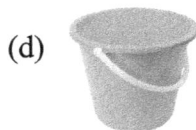

18. Which skeleton is shorter than C?

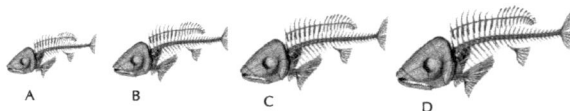

(a) A

(b) B

(c) C

(d) D

19. Which tree is the tallest?

(a) P

(b) Q

(c) R

(d) S

20. Whose balloon has the shortest string?

(a) L

(b) M

(c) N

(d) O

1. Measure the length of the ribbon to the nearest centimetres.

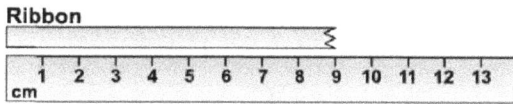

(a) 6   (b) 7

(c) 8   (d) 9

2. Which of the following would you use to hold water?

(a)

(b)

(c)

(d)

3. If each [ ] stands for 1 unit, the weight of clown is _____ units.

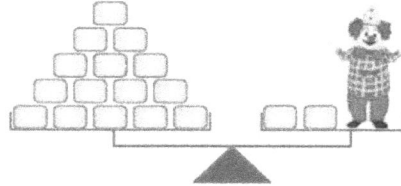

(a) 15 units   (b) 13 units

(c) 12 units   (d) 11 units

4. Look at the boxes carefully.

100kg	50kg	80kg	200kg
A	B	C	D

Box _____ is heavier than box A.

(a) A   (b) B

(c) C   (d) D

5. If weight of Sonu is 30 kg and weight of Arun is more than Sonu, then what is the possible weight of Arun from the following.

(a) 25 kg   (b) 40 kg

(c) 20 kg   (d) 29 kg

1. Tick the shorter.

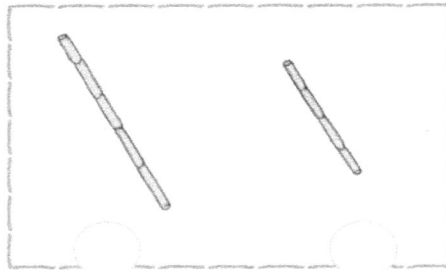

Answer:

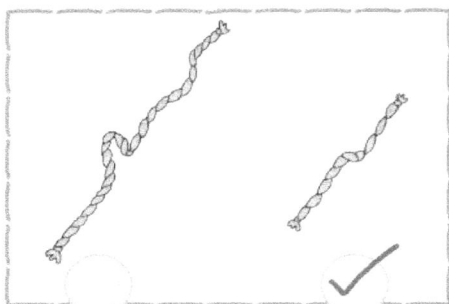

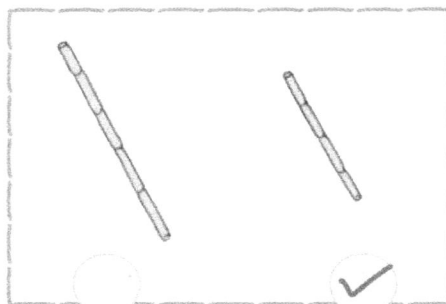

2. Tick the longest.

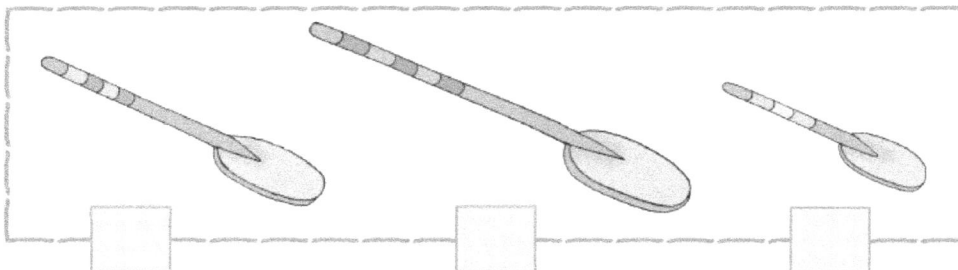

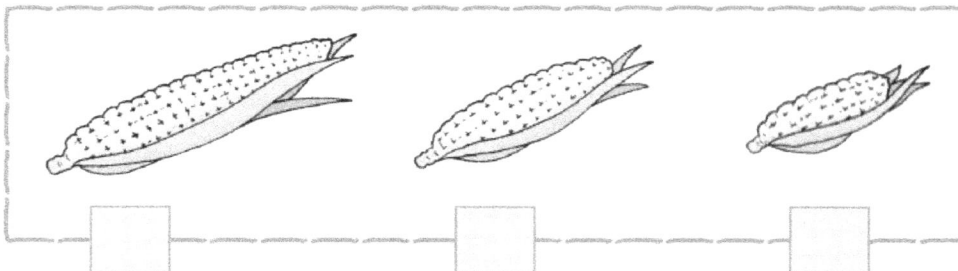

Answer:

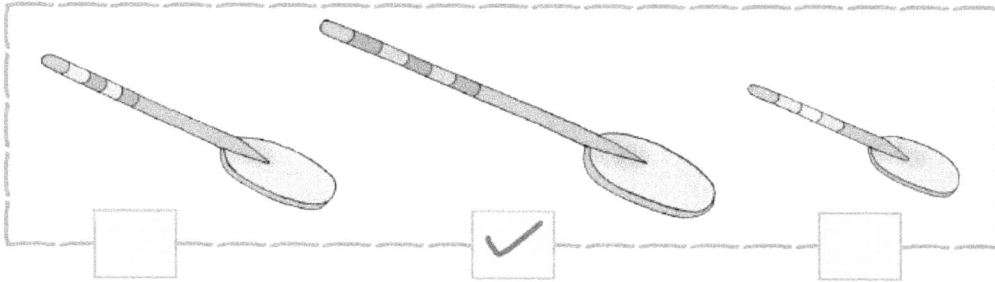

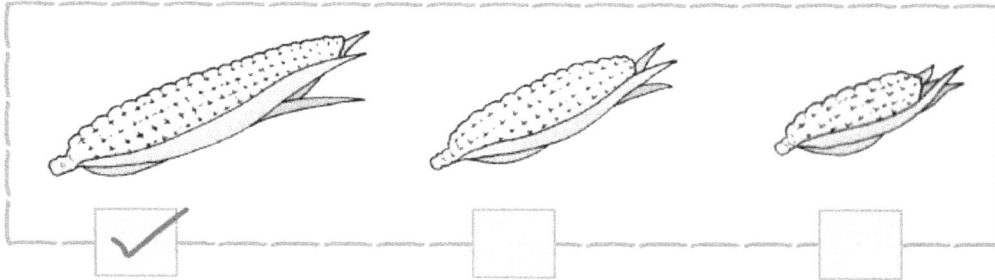

3. Tick the thinner.

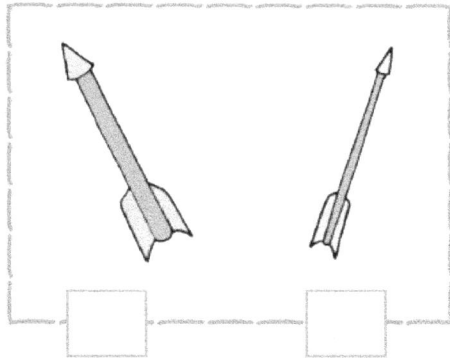

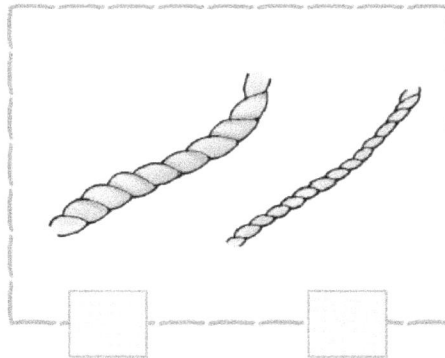

Answer:

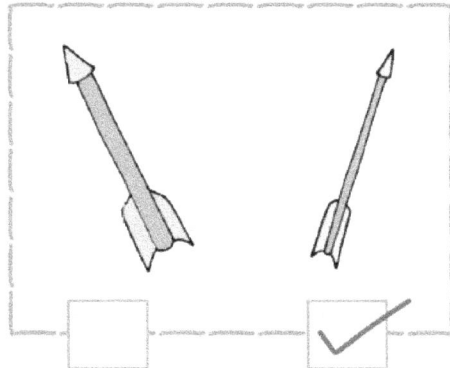

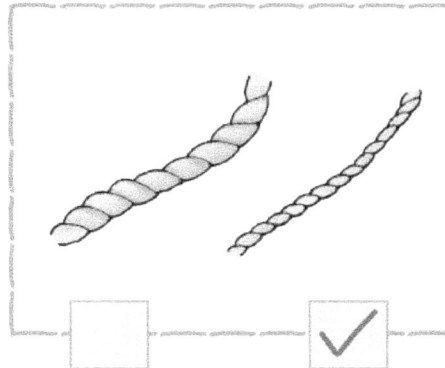

4. Tick the lightest.

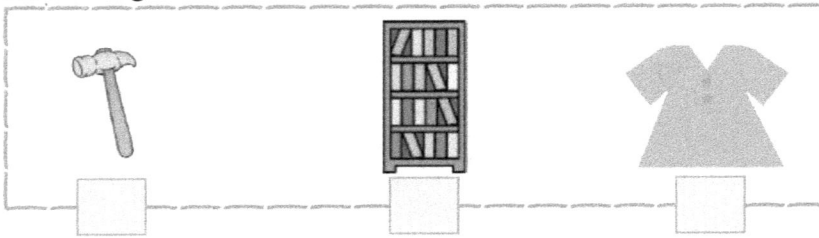

Answer:

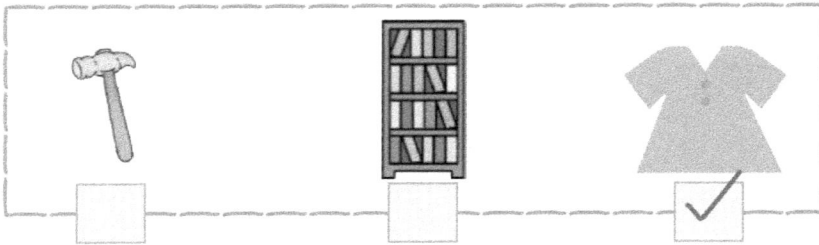

5.

The book is | 3 | spans long.

The table is | | spans long.

Answer:

The book is | 3 | spans long.

The table is | 7 | spans long.

Time

5

Learning Objectives : In this unit, we will learn about:
- ✓ Time
- ✓ Calendar

CHAPTER SUMMARY

Time is measured using a clock. A clock has numbers 1 to 12 on its face, a short hand called the **hour hand** and a long hand called the **minute hand**.

Which Hand is Which?

● **Minute**

● **Hour**

The word 'Minute' is biggest.
The Minute hand is biggest.
The word 'Hour' is smallest.
The Hour hand is smallest.

Some clocks have a third hand called the **second hand**.

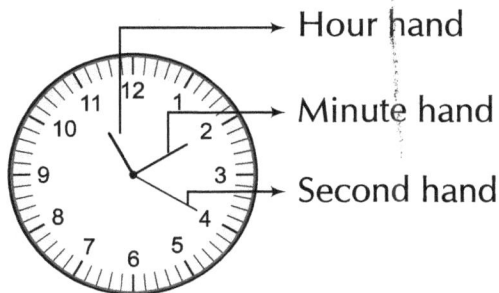

Hour hand

Minute hand

Second hand

Key Points

(i) In 1 hour, the hour hand moves from one number to the next number on the clock.

(ii) In 1 hour, the minute hand goes once around the clock and comes back to its starting position.

(iii) We use 2 dots (:) to separate hours and minutes.

(iv) When the hour hand is at 4 and the minute hand is at 12, the time is read as 4 O' clock or 4 : 00.

(v) 24 hours of a day are divided into day (12 hours) and night (12 hours).

(vi) The time between 12'O clock in the midnight and 12'O clock in the day is called forenoon.

(vii) The time between 12'O clock in the day and 12'O clock in the night is called afternoon. (At 12'O clock it is noon).

TRIVIA

A 'jiffy' is an actual unit of time for 1/100th of a second

Yesterday, Today and Tomorrow

Sunday ⟵ Monday ⟶ Tuesday

Yesterday   Today   Tomorrow

Days of Week

There are seven days in a week.

Monday, Tuesday, Wednesday, Thursday, Friday, Saturday, Sunday

Calender and Months of a Year

Calender : It is a chart which shows days, weeks and months of a year. There are 12 months in a year.

S.No.	Name of Month	No. of Days
1.	January	31
2.	February	28
3.	March	31
4.	April	30
5.	May	31
6.	June	30
7.	July	31
8.	August	31
9.	September	30
10.	October	31
11.	November	30
12.	December	31

Note :

1. There are seven months which have 31 days each.

2. There are four months which have 30 days each.

3. February is the only month which has 28/29 days.

   The year in which February has 29 days is called a leap year.

   1 Year = 365 Days

   1 Leap Year = 366 Days

MUST REMEMBER

➡ A clock has numbers 1 to 12 on its face, a short hand called the hour hand and a long hand called the minute hand.

➡ In 1 hour, the hour hand moves from one number to the next number on the clock.

➡ In 1 hour, the minute hand goes once around the clock and comes back to its starting position.

➡ We use 2 dots (:) to separate hours and minutes.

➡ There are seven months which have 31 days each.

➡ There are four months which have 30 days each.

MULTIPLE CHOICE QUESTIONS

1. What do you do in the evening?
   (a) Play　　　　　(b) Sleep
   (c) Go to school　(d) Eating

2. When do you wake up?
   (a) Afternoon　　(b) Night
   (c) Morning　　　(d) Evening

3. When do you have your breakfast?
   (a) 　(b)
   (c) 　(d)

4. What do you do at night?
   (a) Sleep　　　　(b) Play
   (c) Go to school　(d) Wash clothes

5. Suppose the sun is just above your head. What time of the day is it?
   (a) Morning　　　(b) Noon
   (c) Evening　　　(d) Night

6. Which of the following clocks shows 7'O clock?
   (a) 　(b)
   (c) 　(d)

7. Which of the following clocks shows time less than 5'O clock?
   (a) 　(b)

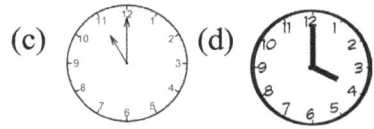

(c) 　(d)

8. Which of the following clocks shows time more than 6'O clock?
   (a) 　(b)
   (c) 　(d)

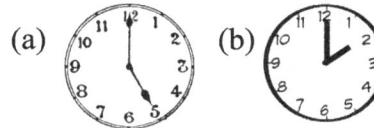

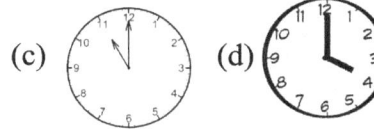

9. Which of these has second hand in the clock?
   (a) 　(b)
   (c) 　(d)

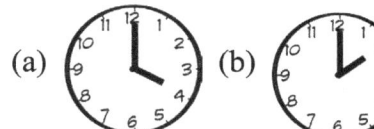

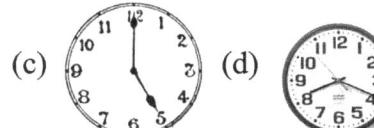

10. Which of the following clocks shows time as 11'O clock?
    (a) 　(b)
    (c) 　(d)

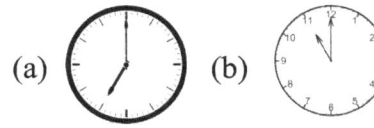

11. If today is Sunday, then tomorrow is _____.

(a) Monday   (b) Saturday

(c) Tuesday   (d) Friday

12. If yesterday was Thursday, then today is _____.

(a) Friday   (b) Wednesday

(c) Saturday   (d) Sunday

13. _____ come after July and before November.

(a) January   (b) December

(c) June   (d) September

14. Which day comes just after Monday?

(a) Sunday   (b) Thursday

(c) Wednesday   (d) Tuesday

15. You play with your friends in playground in _____.

(a) Evening   (b) Night

(c) Morning   (d) Day

16. Which activity you do at night?

(a) Sleeping

(b) Bathing

(c) Playing

(d) Washing

17. We wake up to go to school in

(a) Evening   (b) Night

(c) Morning   (d) Day

18. Which activity you do in morning?

(a) Bathing

(b) Playing

(c) Dinner

(d) Sleeping

19. We go to bed at_____.

(a) Day   (b) Night

(c) Afternoon   (d) Morning

20. Where should be the hour hand and minute hand if it is 6'o clock?

(a) The hour hand on 6 and minute hand on 10

(b) The hour hand on 6 and minute hand on 6

(c) The hour hand on 6 and minute hand on 12

(d) Hour hand on 6 and minute hand on 1

HOTS

1. Which date is the third Saturday of July 20XX?

July 20XX						
S	M	T	W	T	F	S
					1	2
3	4	5	6	7	8	9
10	11	12	13	14	15	16
17	18	19	20	21	22	23
24	25	26	27	28	29	30
31						

(a) July 10   (b) July 16
(c) July 23   (d) July 30

2. How many days are there in 3 weeks?
(a) 14 days   (b) 7 days
(c) 13 days   (d) 21 days

3. How many months of a year has 31 days?
(a) 7   (b) 6
(c) 5   (d) 8

4. What is the 8th month of the year?

(a) July   (b) October
(c) August   (d) September

5. Which of the following months comes just before the ninth month of a year?
(a) August   (b) September
(c) October   (d) July

SUBJECTIVE QUESTIONS

1. Tick the activities that you do in the morning.

Answer:

2. Tick the activities that you do in the evening.

Answer:

3. Number the activities in sequence.

Answer:

5. Tick the activity that will take longer.

Answer:

Money

Learning Objectives : In this unit, we will learn about:
- ✓ Key Points on Money

CHAPTER SUMMARY

Money is used for buying the things we need. In India, money is counted in rupees and paise.

We write ₹ for rupees and p for paise.

Key Points on Money

(i) Symbol of Indian rupees is :

₹

(ii) Money in India comes in form of paper as well as coins.

(iii) 1 Rupee = 100 paise

Following figure shows 100 and 1000 rupees.

₹ 100

₹ 1000

(iv) We write one rupee as ₹ 1.

(v) The paper based notes available in India are of ₹ 2000, ₹ 500, ₹ 200, ₹ 100, ₹ 50, ₹ 20, ₹ 10, ₹ 5 as shown ahead.

(vi) Till few years back there were paper notes for ₹ 2 and ₹ 1 as well but they are no longer in use but, are still valid. Their picture is as shown below :

(vii) The coins available in India are of ₹ 10, ₹ 5, ₹ 2 and ₹ 1 as shown below :

A coin has two sides : a head and a tail.

Tail   Head

Combination of Different Amounts

Different combinations make different amounts of money.

Example :

1 rupee + 1 rupee = 2 rupees

Another example, this time for currency

Notes :

or ₹ 10 + ₹ 10 + ₹ 10 + ₹ 10 + ₹ 10 + ₹ 10 + ₹ 10 + ₹ 10 + ₹ 10 + ₹ 10 = ₹ 100

TRIVIA

Paper money was first used in China over 1000 years ago.

MUST REMEMBER

➡ Money is used for buying the things we need. In India, money is counted in rupees and paise.
➡ Money in India comes in form of paper as well as coins.

MULTIPLE CHOICE QUESTIONS

1. Which has maximum cost?

   (a)  ₹ 55

   (b) 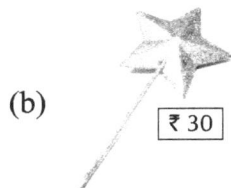 ₹ 30

   (c) 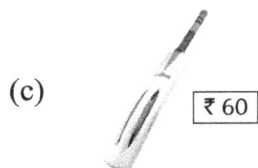 ₹ 60

   (d)  ₹45

2. Which has minimum cost?

   (a) 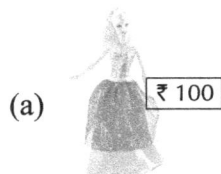 ₹ 100

   (b)  ₹ 150

   (c) 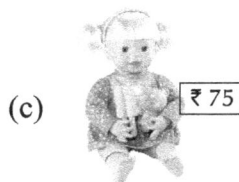 ₹ 75

   (d)  ₹ 30

3. Which amount is more than ₹ 100?
   (a) ₹ 20   (b) ₹ 100
   (c) ₹ 500   (d) ₹ 50 + ₹ 25

4. Ajay wants to exchange his ₹ 10 with some coins. Which set of coins he can take?

   (a)

   (b)

   (c)

   (d)

5. ₹2 can be taken for _____.

(a)

(b)

(c)

(d)

6. How much money is enough to buy this doll?

(a) ₹ 10   (b) ₹ 30
(c) ₹ 100   (d) ₹ 25

 ₹ 30

7. Sonam has ₹ 100. Which of the following she can buy?

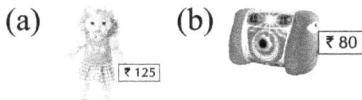

(a) ₹ 125

(b) ₹ 80

(c) ₹150

(d) + ₹ 120

8. ₹ 30 = _____.
(a) Four ₹ 5 coins   (b) Two ₹ 10 coins
(c) Three ₹ 10 coins (d) Three ₹ 5 coins

9. How much amount is shown?

(a) ₹ 10   (b) ₹ 12
(c) ₹ 7   (d) ₹ 15

10. How much amount is shown?

(a) ₹ 155   (b) ₹ 150
(c) ₹ 160   (d) ₹ 170

11. How much money is shown?

(a) ₹ 20   (b) ₹ 22
(c) ₹ 30   (d) ₹ 35

12. Which set of coins shows ₹ 4?

(a)

(b)

(c)

(d)

13. ₹ 6 = ?

(a) +

(b) +

(c) +

(d) +

14. How much amount is shown here?

(a) ₹ 20   (b) ₹ 50
(c) ₹ 2   (d) ₹ 25

15. How much amount is shown here?

(a) ₹ 72   (b) ₹ 60
(c) ₹ 12   (d) ₹ 50

16. Deepak gave ₹ 50 to buy this toy. How much will he get back?
(a) ₹ 10   (b) ₹ 20
(c) ₹ 35   (d) ₹ 30

17. Radha wants to buy . She has ₹ 10. How much more does she need?
(a) ₹ 20   (b) ₹ 15
(c) ₹ 5   (d) ₹ 10

18. ₹10 + ₹10 + ₹10 = _____.
(a) ₹ 35   (b) ₹ 30
(c) ₹ 40   (d) ₹ 20

19. One doll costs ₹ 10. How much money does Priya need to pay for two dolls.
(a) 20   (b) 30
(c) 40   (d) 50

20. Shivam pays ₹ 70 for the and _____ .

(a)   ₹ 30

(b)   ₹ 20

(c)   ₹ 50

(d)   ₹ 50

HOTS

1. If one pencil costs ₹10. How many pencils Riya can buy for ₹20.
   (a) 1   (b) 2
   (c) 3   (d) 4
2. Tanu has ₹50. She buy 2 pens and 1 pencil. Each pen cost ₹10 and cost of a pencil is ₹5. How much money is left with her now?
   (a) 30   (b) 25
   (c) 35   (d) 40
3. Which statement is incorrect .
   (a) ₹100 is more than ₹50
   (b) ₹50 + ₹250 = ₹300
   (c) ₹200 is twice of ₹100
   (d) ₹70 is less than ₹50

4. ₹100 – ₹ _____ = ₹60
   (a) ₹60   (b) ₹40
   (c) ₹30   (d) ₹50
5. Rohan has ₹100. How many cars he can buy from this money.

₹25
   (a) 3   (b) 4
   (c) 2   (d) 1

SUBJECTIVE QUESTIONS

1. Raghu has following money in his Piggy Bank. Count the money.

Answer:
₹ 10 + ₹ 2 + ₹ 2 + ₹ 1 = ₹ 15.

2. Meenu wants to buy a bag worth ₹ 200. She has ₹ 150. How much more money does she need to buy the bag?

Answer:
Bag cost ₹ 200, she has ₹ 150, ₹ 200 – ₹ 150 = ₹ 50. Therefore she needs ₹ 50 more to purchase the bag.

3. Ravi purchased 2 pencils worth ₹ 8, crayons worth ₹ 10 and a notebook worth ₹ 20. How much money in total he spent on purchasing these items?

Answer:

Cost of 2 pencil = ₹ 8 and cost of crayons = ₹ 10 Cost of notebook = ₹ 20. The total amount he spent ₹ 8 + ₹ 10 + ₹ 20 = ₹ 38.

4. How much will 6 oranges, 5 bananas cost?

₹ 6   ₹ 4

Answer:

Price of 1 orange = ₹ 6 Price of 6 oranges = ₹ 6 + 6 + 6 + 6 + 6 + 6 = ₹ 36. Price of 1 banana = ₹ 4. Price of 5 banana = ₹ 4 + 4 + 4 + 4 + 4 = ₹ 20 ₹ 36 + ₹ 20 = Rs.56.

5. Rita went to a shop. She had ₹ 10 with her. She purchased one pencil of ₹ 2 and 2 erasers worth ₹ 4. How much money is left with Rita?

Answer:

Total amount of money she had = ₹ 10 Cost of one pencil = ₹ 2. Cost of two eraser = ₹ 4 Total Cost = (₹ 2 + ₹ 4) = ₹ 6 Money left with Rita = ₹ 10 – ₹ 6 = ₹ 4.

Geometrical Shapes

7

Learning Objectives : In this unit, we will learn about:
- ✓ Plane Shapes
- ✓ Solid Shapes

CHAPTER SUMMARY

Plane Shapes

Shapes like squares, rectangles, circles, triangles and ovals are called **plane shapes**.

Square

A square has 4 sides and 4 corners. All its sides have the same length.

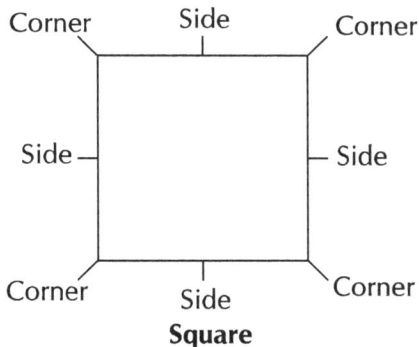

Corner — Side — Corner

Side — Side

Corner — Side — Corner

Square

Rectangle

A rectangle also has 4 sides and 4 corners. Its opposite sides have the same length.

Rectangle

Triangle

A triangle has 3 sides and 3 corners. The three sides of the triangle may or may not be of the same length.

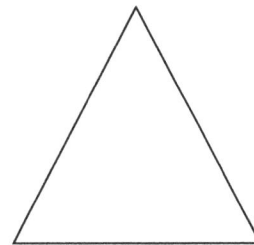

Triangle

Circle

A circle has no sides or corners. It has radius, diameter and circumference.

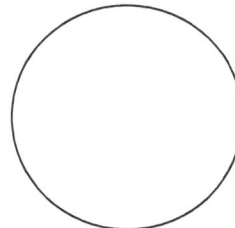

Circle

Oval

An oval also has no sides or corners.

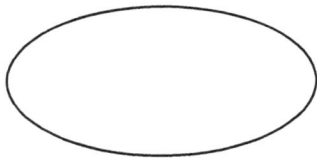

Oval

Solid Shapes

Shapes like cube, cuboid, cylinder, sphere and cone are called **solid shapes**.

Cube

It has 6 equal flat surfaces.

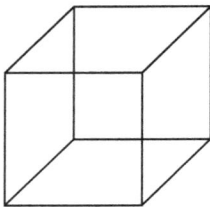

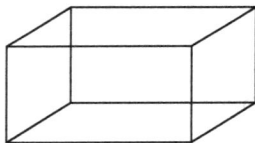

Flat Surface

Cube

Cuboid

It has 6 flat surfaces.

Flat Surface

Cuboid

Cylinder

It has 2 flat faces and 1 curved face.

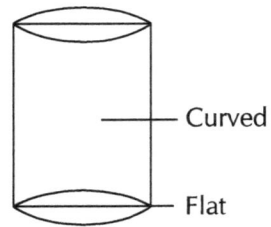

Curved

Flat

Cylinder

Sphere

It has only 1 curved face.

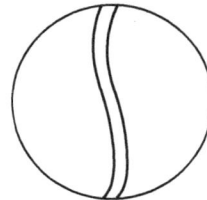

Sphere

Cone

It has one curved face and one flat face.

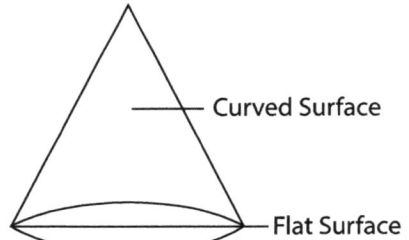

Curved Surface

Flat Surface

Cone

TRIVIA

An icosagon is a shape with 20 sides

➡ A square has 4 sides and 4 corners. All its sides have the same length.

➡ A triangle has 3 sides and 3 corners. The three sides of the triangle may or may not be of the same length.

➡ Shapes like cube, cuboid, cylinder, sphere and cone are called solid shapes.

1. Which object is on the chair?

   (a) (b)

   (c) (d)

2. How many circles are there in the figure?

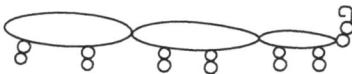

   (a) 12   (b) 11
   (c) 14   (d) 15

3. Which objects are outside the box?

   (a)

   (b)

   (c)

   (d)

4. Which shape is a triangle?

   (a)

   (b)

   (c)

   (d)

5. Which of the following looks like a cube?

   (a)   (b)

   (c)   (d)

6. How many circles are there in the box?

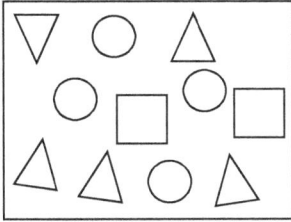

(a) 6   (b)5
(c) 7   (d) 4

7. Name the shape which is shaded below.

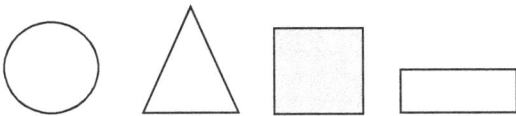

(a) Triangle   (b) Square
(c) Rectangle   (d) Circle

8. Name the shape of the shaded part ....

(a) Rectangle   (b) Triangle
(c) Circle   (d) Square

9. How many circles are there inside the big circle?

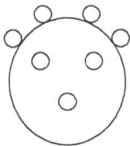

(a) 4   (b) 3
(c) 5   (d) 2

10. There are .... more circles (○) in the clown's cap than the face.

(a) 2   (b) 3
(c) 1   (d) 0

11. Arrange the given balls from the biggest to the smallest?

(a) L, M, N, O   (b) M, N, L, O
(c) O, L, N, M   (d) M, N, O, L

12. Select the correct match of the shapes that can be drawn, using given solid objects along these.

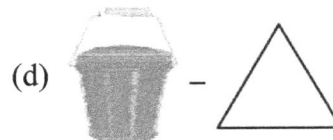

(a)

(b)

(c)

(d)

13. In which of the following group(s) the shape can be placed?

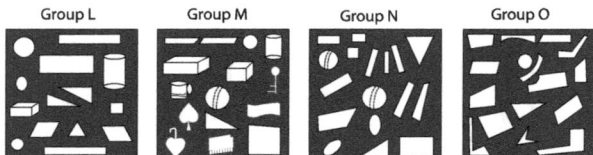

Group L   Group M   Group N   Group O

(a) Both L and M
(b) Only L
(c) Only M
(d) L, M, N and O

14. Which figure is not shown below?

(a) Rectangle   (b) Triangle
(c) Square   (d) Circle

15. Count the total number of triangles.

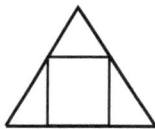

(a) 3   (b) 4
(c) 2   (d) 1

16. Amit has 4 groups of shapes.

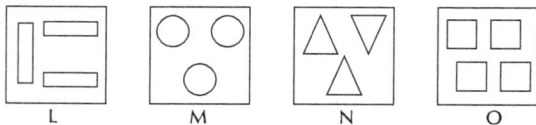

In which group he will put a ring?
(a) L   (b) M
(c) N   (d) O

17. What is the shape of a slice of the pizza?

(a) Rectangle   (b) Triangle
(c) Square   (d) Circle

18. Tanu draws a figure which consists of three triangles and one circle. Which of the following could be Tanu's drawing?

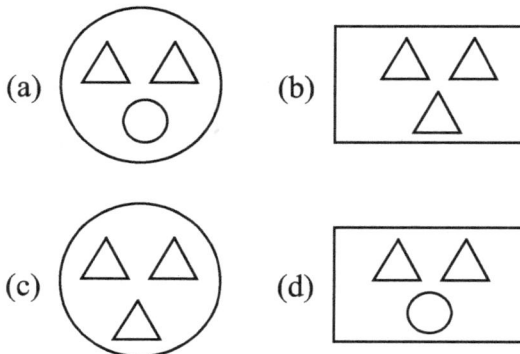

19. What is the shape of a dice?
(a) Cylinder   (b) Cube
(c) Cone   (d) Sphere

20. The rocket below is a combination of a _____ and a _____.

(a) Cuboid, Sphere   (b) Cone, Cube
(c) Cube, Cylinder (d) Cone, Cylinder

1. Identify the object which is under the table and rolling also.

    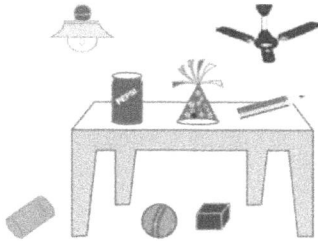

    (a)

    (b)

    (c)

    (d)

2. Count the total number of squares.

    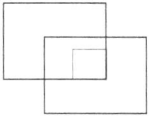

    (a) 2   (b) 3
    (c) 1   (d) 4

3. How many different types of shapes are there in the given figure?

    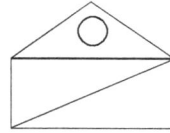

    (a) 3   (b) 2
    (c) 1   (d) 4

4. What is the shape of the surfaces of a cuboid?

    (a) Circle   (b) Rectangle
    (c) Triangle   (d) Oval

5. Match the following :

Shape	Numbers of sides
(A) Square	(i) 12
(B) Circle	(ii) 4
(C) Triangle	(iii) 0
(D) Cube	(iv) 3

    (a) (A)→(ii); (B) →(iii); (C) →(iv); (D) →(i)
    (b) (A) →(iii); (B) →(ii); (C) →(i); (D) →(iv)
    (c) (A)→(ii); (B)→(i); (C)→(iii); (D)→(iv)
    (d) (A) →(i); (B)→(ii); (C)→(iii); (D)→(iv)

1. How many lines are required to make 2 square?
    Answer:
    One square has 4 lines.
    So 4 + 4 = 8 lines are required to make 2 squares.

2. Match similar shapes by drawing a line.

    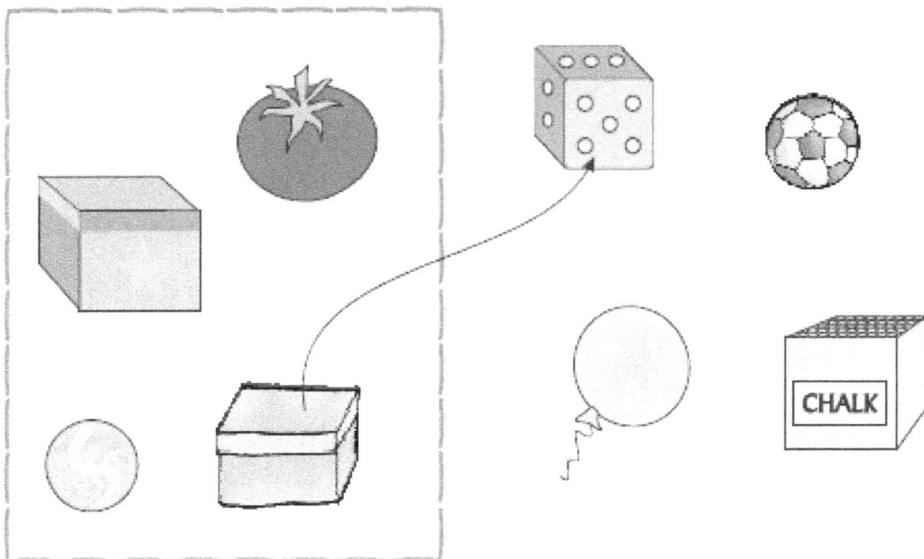

    Answer:

    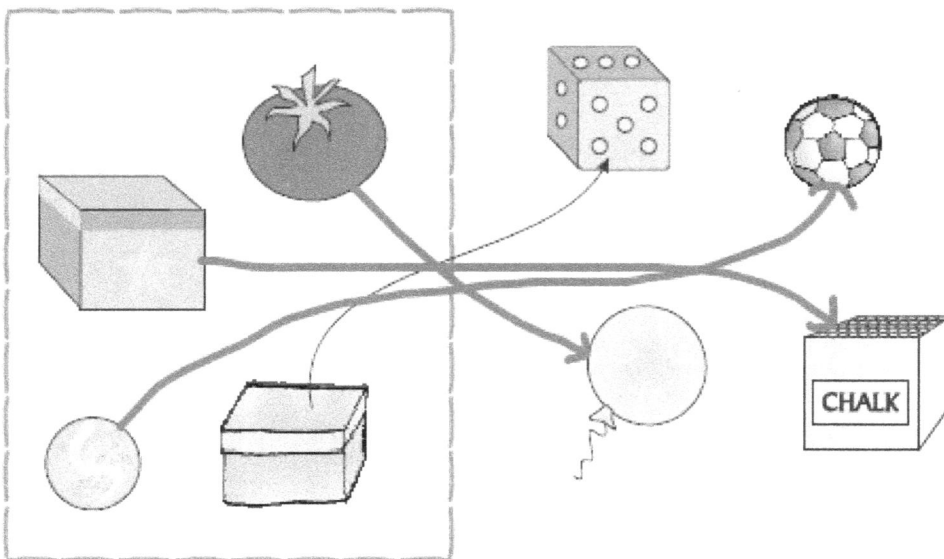

3. Tick (✓) the objects that will roll.

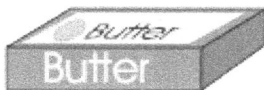

Answer:

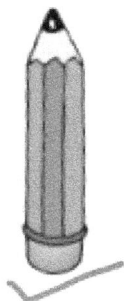

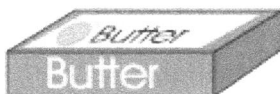

4. Tick (✓) the objects that will slide.

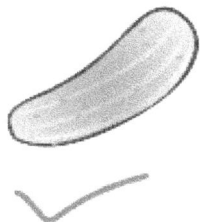

Answer:

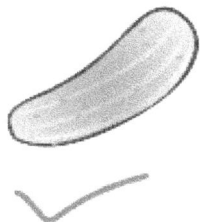

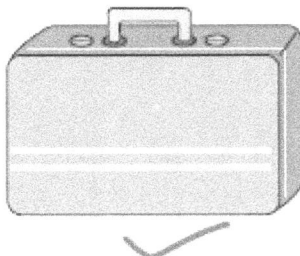

5. Match the shapes of the same sizes.

Answer:

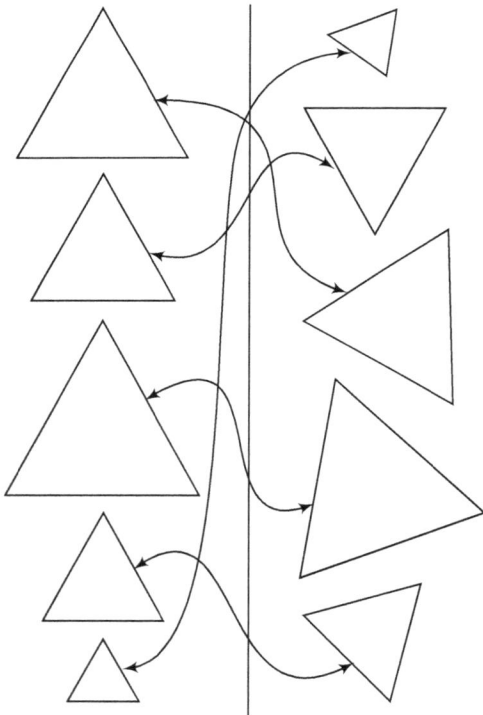

SECTION 2
LOGICAL REASONING

Patterns

1

> **Learning Objectives :** In this unit, we will learn about:
> ✓ The concept of patterns
> ✓ Types of patterns

CHAPTER SUMMARY

Pattern is a repeated sequence of letters, numbers and shapes, which has a particular logical design. Patterns can be classified as follows:

1. Identification of missing number in the number series or missing letters in the letter series pattern.

   Example : 10, 22, 34, 46, 58......

   Solution : The pattern followed in the above example is addition of 12 in each number to get the next number.

2. Identification of missing part in a figure.

   Example :

(a)   (b)

(c)   (d)

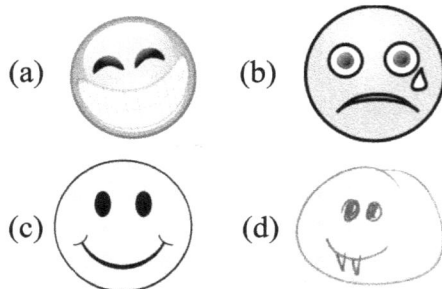

Solution : Answer is option (b) In the above series, smileys follow normal to extreme facial expressions.

1. Find the missing number in the given number pattern, if the series in both the patterns follows the same rule.

Pattern I	Pattern II
22	60
30	68
38	?

(a) 76   (b) 66
(c) 36   (d) 56

2. Find the missing number in the given number pattern.

80, 70, 55, 45, ?

(a) 25   (b) 30
(c) 20   (d) 35

3. Complete the pattern by choosing the next figure.

(a)   (b)

(c)   (d)

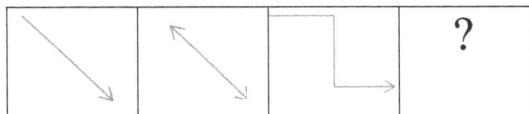

4. Complete the pattern by choosing the next figure.

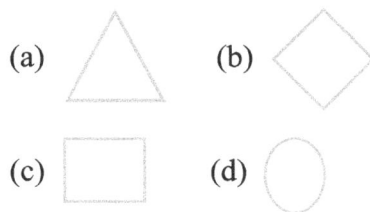

(a)   (b)

(c)   (d)

5. Complete the pattern by choosing the next figure.

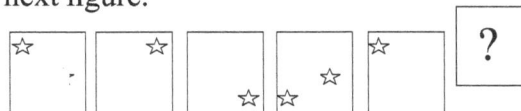

(a)   (b)

(c)   (d)

6. Find the missing number in the given number pattern.

428, 418, 430, ?, 432, 422, 434, ?

(a) 418, 436   (b) 422, 444
(c) 420, 446   (d) 420, 424

7. Which of the following replaces the question mark (?) in given number patterns?

(a) 43   (b) 42
(c) 35   (d) 13

8. Complete the number pattern given below.

16, 20, 24, 28, ?

(a) 40   (b) 10
(c) 32   (d) 36

9. Complete the pattern by choosing the next figure.

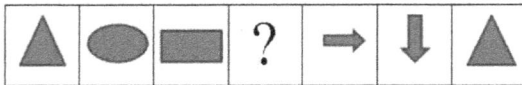

(a)

(b)

(c)

(d)

10. Complete the pattern by choosing the next figure.

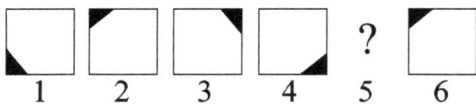

(a)

(b)

(c)

(d)

11. Complete the pattern by filling the boxes.

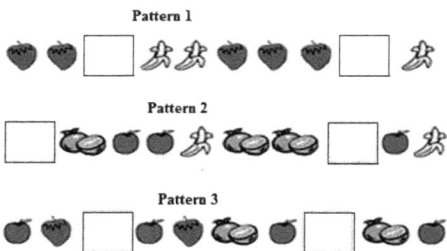

Pattern 1

Pattern 2

Pattern 3

(a) Pattern 1 : ; Pattern 2 : Pattern 3 :

(b) Pattern 1 : ; Pattern 2 : Pattern 3 :

(c) Pattern 1 : ; Pattern 2 : Pattern 3 :

(d) Pattern 1 : ; Pattern 2 : Pattern 3 :

12. What comes next in the alphabetical pattern?

ACE, GIK, MOQ, ?
(a) ABE   (b) RQT
(c) RTW   (d) SUW

13. Complete the pattern by choosing the next figure.

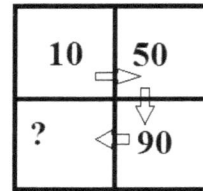

(a) 120   (b) 130
(c) 140   (d) 150

14. Which of the following replaces the question mark (?) in given number patterns?

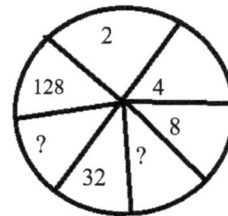

(a) 24, 16   (b) 16, 64
(c) 44, 64   (d) 64, 24

15. What comes next in the alphabetical pattern?

J K L D K L J K L D K L J K L D K L J ?
(a) D   (b) L
(c) K   (d) J

16. How many ants will be there in pattern 3?

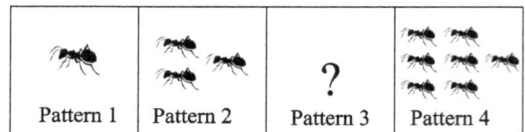

(a) 4   (b) 6
(c) 8   (d) 5

17. Which of the following replaces the question mark (?) in given pattern?

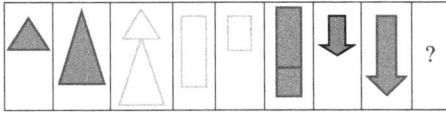

(a)   (b)   (c)   (d)

18. Which of the following replaces the question mark (?) in given number patterns?

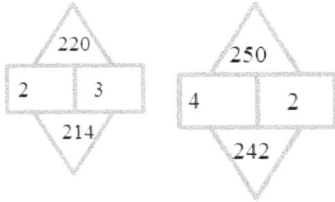

(a) 357   (b) 362
(c) 338   (d) 346

19. Look at the given pattern.

How would you show this pattern using letters?
(a) AAVVAAA   (b) TTTVTTT
(c) VVTTTVV   (d) VTTTVTTT

20. If A = 1, B = 2, C = 3, D = 4, and so on then find B + C.
(a) E   (b) L
(c) J   (d) G

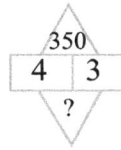

Odd One Out

2

Learning Objectives : In this unit, we will learn about:
- ✓ Odd One Out (Classification)
- ✓ Steps to solve problems

CHAPTER SUMMARY

Classification

In such problems, we are given a set of figures or alphabets or numbers. Among these all have some common things except one. We are required to select the option which differs from all others in the given set.

The following steps can help you to solve these problems easily.

Step 1 : Look for common things in each option.

Step 2 : Find a pattern in the similarities.

Step 3 : Which one is different and why.

Note : Make sure to verify that your chosen answer does not match the group in any way.

Example : Which one is odd one out?

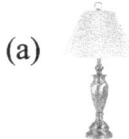

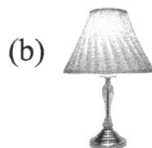

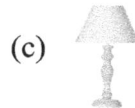

(a)

(b)

(c)

(d)

Solution :

Step 1 : What is each object for?
To give light.

Step 2 : Where is each object found?
- (a) On the table
- (b) On the table
- (c) On the table
- (d) On the ceiling

Step 3 : Is there a common feature? Yes, on the table.

Step 4 : Is there an odd one out? Yes, to the ceiling. So answer is (d)

1. Find the odd one out.

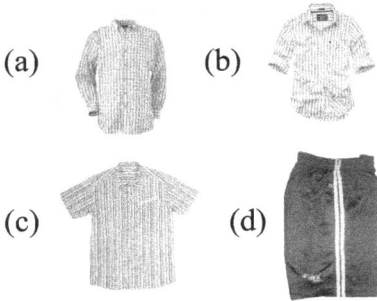

    (a)   (b)

    (c)   (d)

2. Find the odd one out.

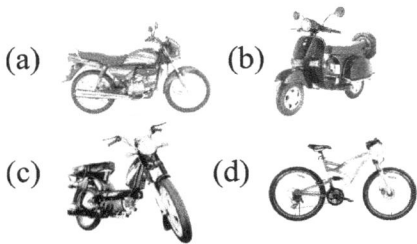

    (a)   (b)

    (c)   (d)

3. Find the odd one out.

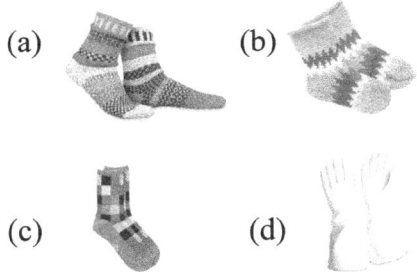

    (a)   (b)

    (c)   (d)

4. Find the odd one out.

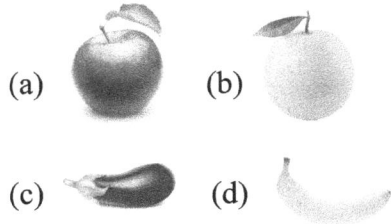

    (a)   (b)

    (c)   (d)

5. Find the odd one out.
    (a) 2   (b) 4
    (c) 21   (d) A

6. Find the odd one out.
    (a) Pencil   (b) Clock
    (c) Eraser   (d) Sharpener

7. Find the odd one out.
    (a) Dress   (b) Bat
    (c) Ball   (d) Wicket

8. Find the odd one out.

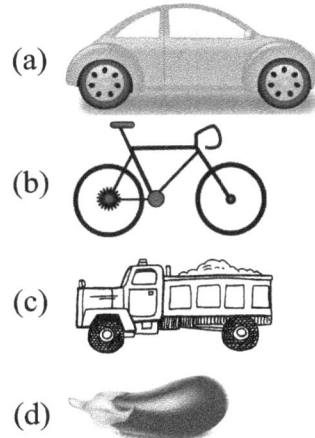

    (a)

    (b)

    (c)

    (d)

9. Find the odd one out.

    (a)   (b)

    (c)   (d)

10. Find the odd one out.

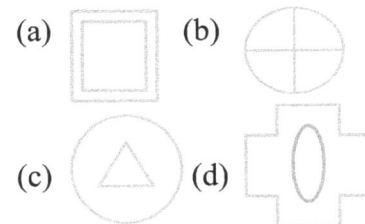

    (a)   (b)

    (c)   (d)

11. Find the odd one out.

16, 20, 24, 28, 32, 38, 40

(a) 20   (b) 28
(c) 33   (d) 38

12. Find the odd one out.

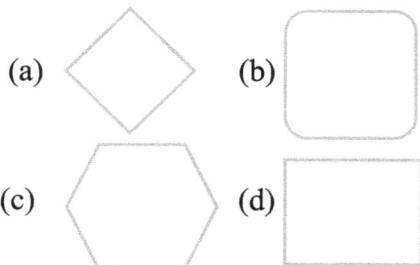

(a)   (b)

(c)   (d)

13. Find the odd one out.

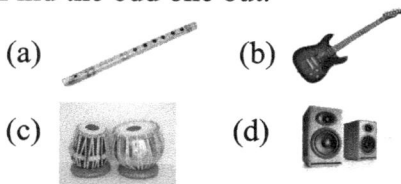

(a)   (b)

(c)   (d)

14. Find the odd one.

(a)   (b)

(c)   (d)

15. Find odd one out.

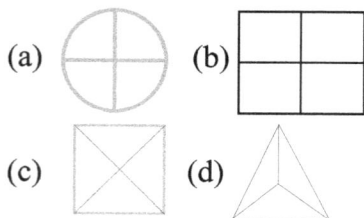

(a)   (b)

(c)   (d)

16. Look at the following pictures carefully and choose odd one out.

(a)   (b)

(c)   (d)

17. Find odd one out.

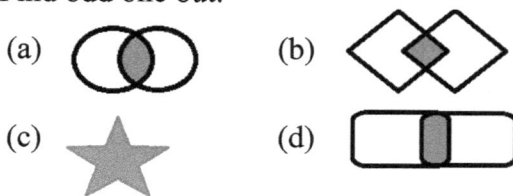

(a)   (b)

(c)   (d)

18. Find the odd one.

72, 36, 18, 6, 4.5
(a) 4.5   (b) 6
(c) 3   (d) 18

19. Find the odd one.

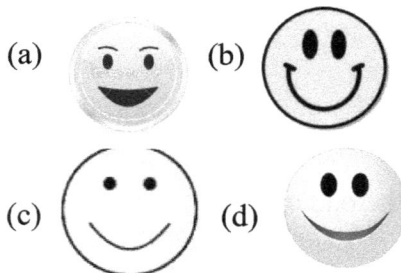

(a)   (b)

(c)   (d)

20. Find odd one out.

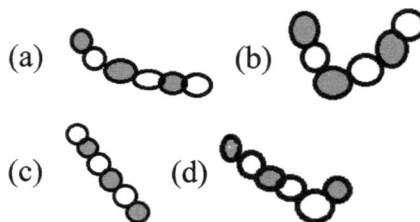

(a)   (b)

(c)   (d)

Analogy

3

Learning Objectives : In this unit, we will learn about:
- ✓ The concept of analogy
- ✓ Examples on analogy

CHAPTER SUMMARY

Analogy means a comparison between two things that have some relationship on the basis of their similarities.

In these types of questions, we have to find out the relation among different options.

Example 1 : Find out the relation.

Text : Paper :: Paper : ?

(a) Pen   (b) Book

(c) Ink   (d) Pencil

Solution : As text is found in paper similarly paper is found in book. So the answer is (b).

Example 2 : Find the missing shape by identifying the relationship.

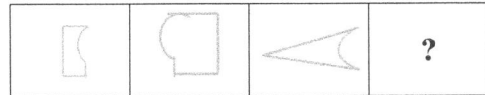

(a)   (b)

(c)   (d)

Solution : In the figure, the curved part comes outwards and the pattern is reversed. So the answer is (c).

1. Find out the relation.

   Month : 30 :: Week : ?

   (a) 10   (b) 7

   (c) 11   (d) 15

2. Find out the relation.
   Bread : Butter :: Tea : ?

   (a) Snacks   (b) Pizza

   (c) Coffee   (d) Milk

3. Find the missing shape by identifying the relationship.

   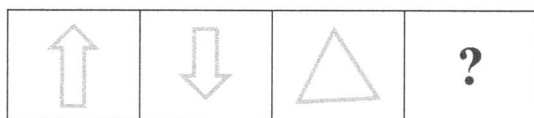

   (a)   (b)

   (c)   (d)

4. Find the missing shape by identifying the relationship.

   (a)   (b)

   (c)   (d)

5. Find out the relation.
   Father : Mother : : Grandfather : ?

   (a) Grandson   (b) Daughter

   (c) Grandmother   (d) Granddaughter

6. Find out the relation.
   Fingers : Hands : :Teeth : ?

   (a) Heart   (b) Stomach

   (c) Palm   (d) Mouth

7. Find the missing shape by identifying the relationship.

   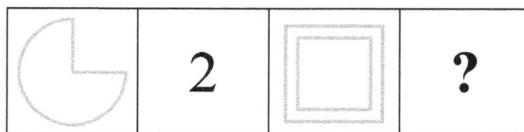

   (a) 8   (b) 4

   (c) 6   (d) 10

8. Find the missing shape by identifying the relationship.

   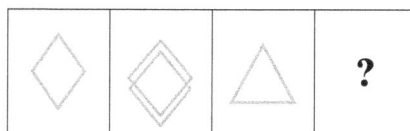

   (a)   (b)

   (c)   (d)

9. Find the missing shape by identifying the relationship.

   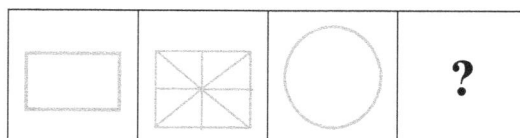

   (a)   (b)

   (c)   (d)

10. Find the missing shape by identifying the relationship.

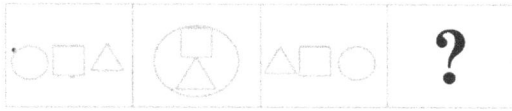

(a)

(b)

(c)

(d)

11. Find the missing shape by identifying the relationship.

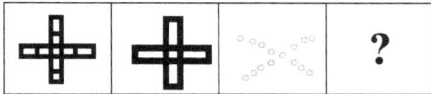

(a)

(b)

(c)

(d)

12. Find the missing shape by identifying the relationship.

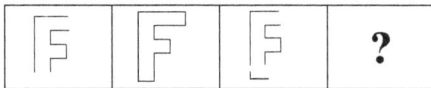

(a)

(b)

(c)

(d)

Directions (13–16): Choose the word which best completes each analogy.

13. Elbow is to hand as fingers are to_____.
    (a) Feet
    (b) Palm
    (c) Leg
    (d) Body

14. A dolphin is to sea as a chicken is to _____ .
    (a) Burrow
    (b) Stable
    (c) Hive
    (d) Coop

15. A week is to 7 days as an hour is to _____minutes.
    (a) 60 min
    (b) 100 min
    (c) 80 min
    (d) 3600 min

16. Bark is to tree as skin is to _____.
    (a) Fur
    (b) Human body
    (c) Plastic
    (d) Vegetables

17. Find the missing shape by identifying the relationship.

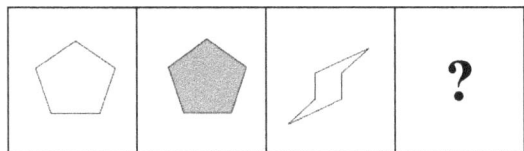

(a)

(b)

(c)

(d)

18. Find the missing shape by identifying the relationship.

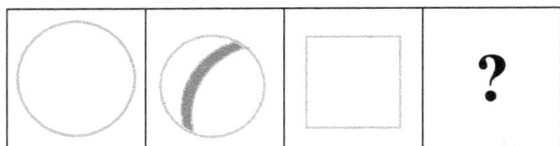

(a)   (b)

(c)   (d)

19. Find the missing shape by identifying the relationship.

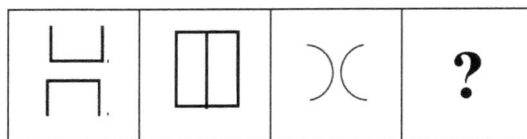

(a)   (b)

(c)   (d)

20. Find the missing word by identifying the relationship.

Guitar : Music :: Food: ?

(a) Energy (b) Run
(c) Jump (d) Rest

Ranking Test

Learning Objectives : In this unit, we will learn about:
- ✓ The concept of Ranking Test
- ✓ Types of Ranking Test

CHAPTER SUMMARY

Ranking is based on the arrangement of different things like, persons, objects or characters based on some special feature in a specific order.

Ranking test can be of various categories:

1. In the first category, position or rank of an object or a person is identified from left end or right end or from top or bottom.

2. Second category is based on interchanging of the positions of two persons or objects.

3. Third category is based on the position of any person or object with respect to other person or object.

4. Fourth category is based on the identification of position or object after removing some of the objects in the series.

Example : Observe the following figures carefully.

Left First

a   b   c   d

e   f   g   h

Right Last

Apple 'd' is at the fourth position and is the immediate left of the apple_____.

(a) c   (b) e

(c) a   (d) f

Solution :

Apple 'd' is at the 4th position and it is the immediate left to the e apple. So answer is (b).

Example : Observe the given figures carefully :

If Summi's position is interchanged by Somya's postion, then which girl will be positioned at 6th position?

(a) Somya   (b) Summi

(c) Somi   (d) Sonu

Answer (c)

Example : If the right most apple is eaten by someone, which apple will become the fifth from the right end?

Left

Right

(a) H   (b) G

(c) C   (d) P

Answer (c)

Direction (1-5) : Observe the given figure carefully and answer the following questions.

Left (first)

P   N   I   K   O   J   M   L

1. Which bird is seventh from the right end?
   (a) M   (b) L
   (c) N   (d) P

2. Bird O is second to the right of bird
   _____.
   (a) P   (b) I
   (c) M   (d) N

3. If bird P and I interchange their positions, then bird _____ is at the left end.
   (a) I   (b) L
   (c) P   (d) M

4. Bird J is just left to _____ bird.
   (a) N   (b) O
   (c) M   (d) L

5. Bird ____ is the sixth bird to the right of bird N.
   (a) J   (b) K
   (c) M   (d) L

Directions (6-10) : Observe the given figure carefully and answer the following questions.

D   J   E   M   K   F   I   L   G   H

Left   Right

6. Which umbrella is 10th from the right end?
   (a) D   (b) H
   (c) J   (d) G

7. If Suhani took the immediate left umbrella of the umbrella K, which umbrella did she take?
   (a) M   (b) N
   (c) F   (d) H

8. Identify the position of the umbrella K from the left.
   (a) Fifth   (b) Sixth
   (c) Ninth   (d) Seventh

9. Umbrella E is __ to the left of umbrella F.
   (a) Second   (b) Fourth
   (c) Fifth   (d) Third

10. Umbrella _____ is the right of umbrella F and left of umbrella L.
    (a) K   (b) I
    (c) L   (d) G

Directions (11-14) : Observe the given figure carefully and answer the following questions.

Left/First

P   Q   T   V   W   R   U   S

11. Brick W is at the 5th position from the left. Now find out the name and position (from the left) of the brick which is at the immediate left of the W brick.
    (a) V, fifth   (b) R, fifth
    (c) V, fourth   (d) R, fourth

12. If brick P and brick U interchange their position, then brick _____ is at the left end.
    (a) Q   (b) U
    (c) P   (d) S

13. Which brick is seventh to the right of brick P?

    (a) S   (b) U

    (c) R   (d) P

14. How many bricks are there between brick P and brick U?

    (a) 5   (b) 8

    (c) 7   (d) 10

Directions (15–16) : Observe the given figures carefully and answer the following questions.

Left/First

Jyoti   Shiva   Reema   Sushma   Meghna   Ananya

15. Sushma is standing between _____ and _____.

    (a) Reema and Ananya

    (b) Meghna and Reema

    (c) Jyoti and Shiva

    (d) Ananya and Shiva

16. If Ananya and Shiva interchange their positions, then Ananya will be at the immediate left of _____.

    (a) Reema   (b) Jyoti

    (c) Meghna   (d) Sushma

17. There are 20 students in a class. Six of them are standing, and 10 of them are sitting in the class. Now find out the number of remaining students in the class.

    (a) 16   (b) 4

    (c) 6   (d) 8

Directions (18–20) : There are 10 rows of students in a class, five students in each row. Rohit is sitting at the 3rd position (from the left) of the fourth row, Sumit is at the 5th position in the same row, and Sneha at the immediate right of Rohit.

18. In which row is Sneha sitting?

    (a) 6th (b) 10th

    (c) 4th (d) 5th

19. In which row, from the back, is Rohit sitting?

    (a) 4th (b) 7th

    (c) 6th (d) 5th

20. If Rohit is sitting at the 8th position from the front, then what will be his position from the end of the row among 20 students?

    (a) 32rd   (b) 13th

    (c) 34th   (d) 20th

Problems Based on Figures

5

Learning Objectives : In this unit, we will learn about:
- ✓ Grouping of Figures
- ✓ Embedded Figures

CHAPTER SUMMARY

Grouping of Figures

In grouping of figures, a set of figures or numbers are grouped on the basis of certain properties or parameters. The basic fundamentals of fractioning, division and multiplication are applied while grouping of figures.

Example : Identify the number of 2's group from the following pictures.

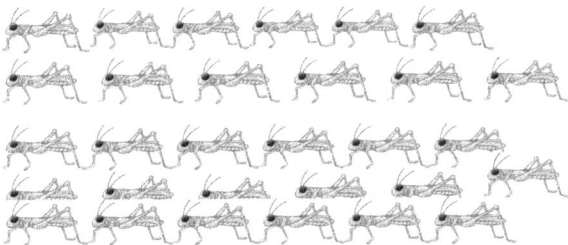

(a) 10   (b) 15
(c) 20   (d) 30

Explanation :

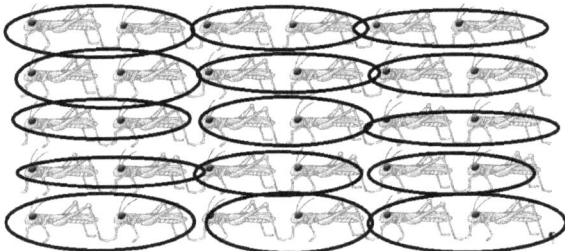

Total 15 groups can be formed.

Example: Number 5 belongs to group _____.

| 5, 15, 30, 100, 21 |
| 33, 10, 13 19, 28 |
| 20, 24, 18, 68, 32 |

Group P

| 4, 7, 12, 18, 24 |
| 28, 7, 9, 38, 42 |
| 9, 36, 64, 63, 59 |

Group Q

| 17, 52, 54, 8, 7 |
| 51, 41, 31, 21, 11 |
| 101, 116, 109, 89, 72 |

Group R

(a) Group R   (b) Group Q
(c) Group P   (d) All the groups

Embedded Figures

When a figure is embossed on another figure, it is said to be an embedded figure. Embedded figures can be divided into two parts.

1. Identification of small hidden part in the given figure.
2. Identification of the main figure in which given part is hidden.

Example 1. Which of the following part is embedded in the given figure?

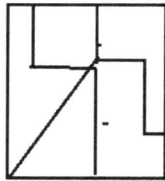

(a) (b)

(c) (d)

Solution : (d)

Example 2. In which of the following figures, is the given shape embedded?

A.   B.   C.   D.

Solution : (d)

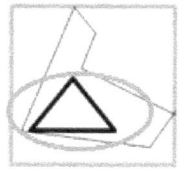

MULTIPLE CHOICE QUESTIONS

1. How many groups of 3-stars are there?

   (a) 24   (b) 3
   (c) 8   (d) 10

2. How many groups of 2 rectangles can be formed from the group of assorted shapes given in the box?

   (a) 1   (b) 2
   (c) 4   (d) 3

3. Identify the group in which components can be divided into groups of four equally and completely.

   A   B   C   D

4. How many groups of 2 giraffes are there?

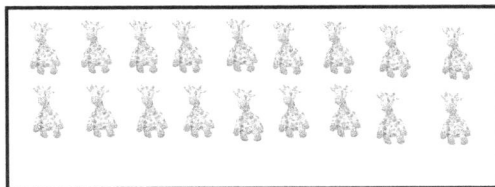

   (a) 10   (b) 9
   (c) 18   (d) 20

5. How many groups of 4 bottles are there?

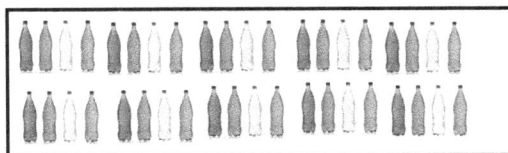

   (a) 10   (b) 5
   (c) 20   (d) 40

6. How many groups of 2 bottles can be formed from given group of bottles?

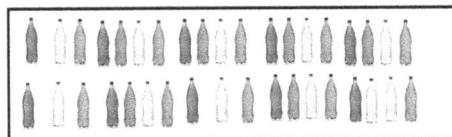

   (a) 19   (b) 10
   (c) 20   (d) 15

7. Shape (A) belongs to group _____.

Shape A

Group W   Group X   Group Y   Group Z

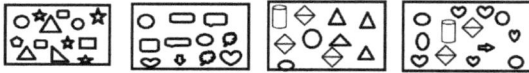

(a) Only W   (b) Only Z
(c) Both W and X   (d) Both W and Y

Direction (8–10) : Observe and study the given figures and choose the correct answer which relates to the given figures.

8.

(a) 8 groups of 2 fish
(b) 2 groups of 5 fish
(c) 3 groups of 5 fish
(d) 2 group of 6 fish

9.

(a) 5 groups of 5   (b) 4 groups of 6
(c) 7 groups of 7   (d) 8 groups of 4

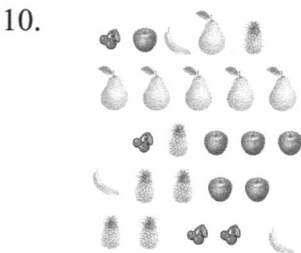

10.

(a) 3 groups of 3 apples and 2 groups of 3 pears
(b) 2 groups of 3 apples, 2 groups of 3 pineapples, and 2 groups of 3 pears
(c) 2 groups of 3 apples, 2 groups of 3 pineapples, 1 group of 3 bananas, and 2 groups of 3 pears
(d) 3 groups of 3 apples, 3 groups of 3 pineapples, 1 group of 3 bananas, and 2 groups of 3 pears

Directions (11-14) : Which of the following figures is hidden or embedded in the given figure?

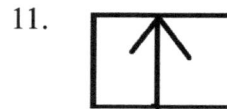

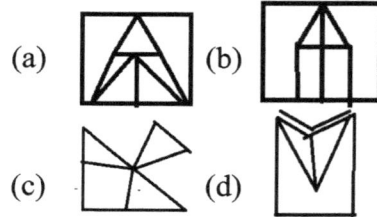

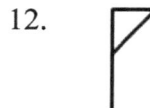

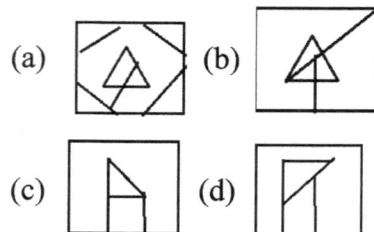

11.

(a)   (b)

(c)   (d)

12.

(a)   (b)

(c)   (d)

13.

(a)  (b)

(c) (d)

14.

(a) (b)

(c) (d)

Directions (15–16) : Find the figure which is not hidden in the given figure.

15.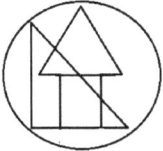

(a) (b)

(c) (d)

16.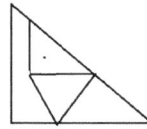

(a) (b)

(c) (d)

Directions (17–20) : In which of the following figures, the given shape (X) is embedded as its part?

17. 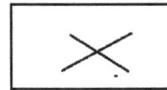 Shape X

(a) (b)

(c) (d)

18. 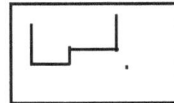 Shape X

(a) (b)

(c) (d)

19.  Shape X

(a)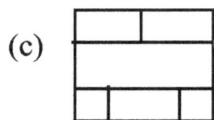

(b)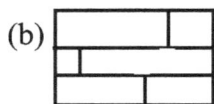

(c)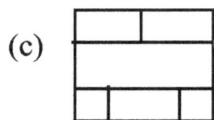

(d)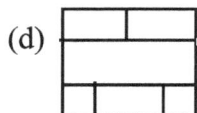

20. 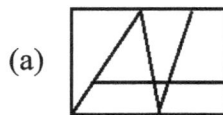 Shape X

(a)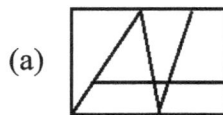

(b)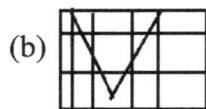

(c)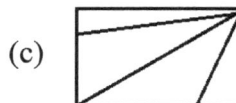

(d)

SECTION 3
ACHIEVERS' SECTION

Some Important Concepts

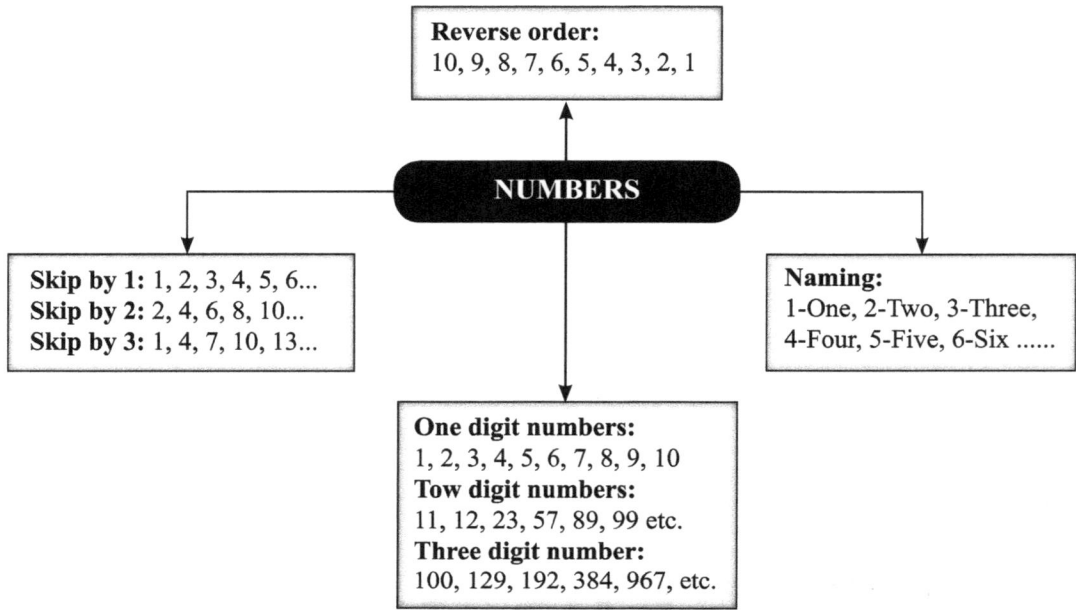

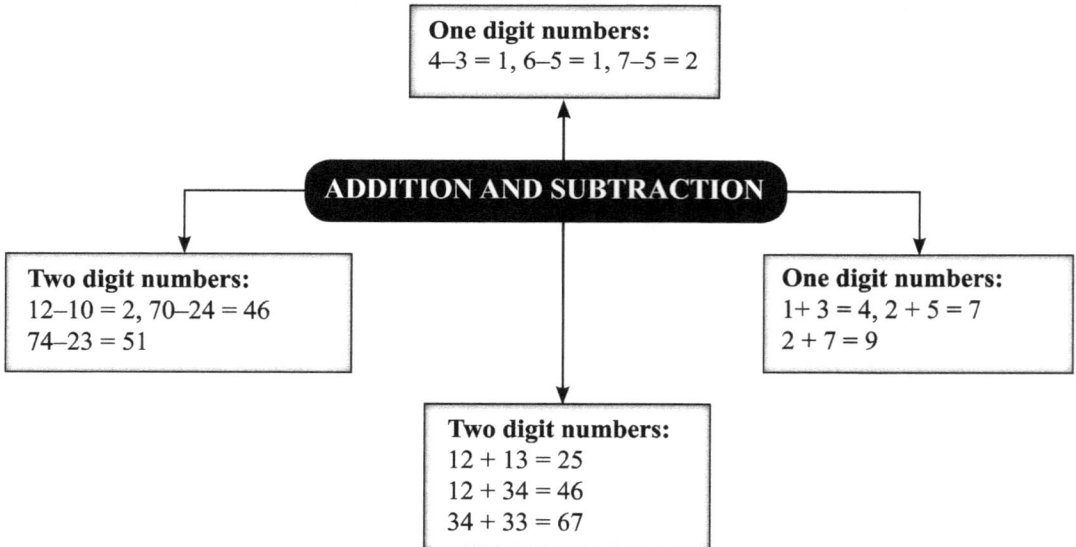

Reverse order:
10, 9, 8, 7, 6, 5, 4, 3, 2, 1

NUMBERS

Skip by 1: 1, 2, 3, 4, 5, 6...
Skip by 2: 2, 4, 6, 8, 10...
Skip by 3: 1, 4, 7, 10, 13...

Naming:
1-One, 2-Two, 3-Three,
4-Four, 5-Five, 6-Six ......

One digit numbers:
1, 2, 3, 4, 5, 6, 7, 8, 9, 10
Tow digit numbers:
11, 12, 23, 57, 89, 99 etc.
Three digit number:
100, 129, 192, 384, 967, etc.

One digit numbers:
4–3 = 1, 6–5 = 1, 7–5 = 2

ADDITION AND SUBTRACTION

Two digit numbers:
12–10 = 2, 70–24 = 46
74–23 = 51

One digit numbers:
1+ 3 = 4, 2 + 5 = 7
2 + 7 = 9

Two digit numbers:
12 + 13 = 25
12 + 34 = 46
34 + 33 = 67

Days of the Week

days of the week (7 days)	weekdays (5 days)	Monday
		Tuesday
		Wednesday
		Thursday
		Friday
	weekend (2 days)	Saturday
		Sunday

Thoughtful Questions

1. Develop a story on the pictures and write about it.

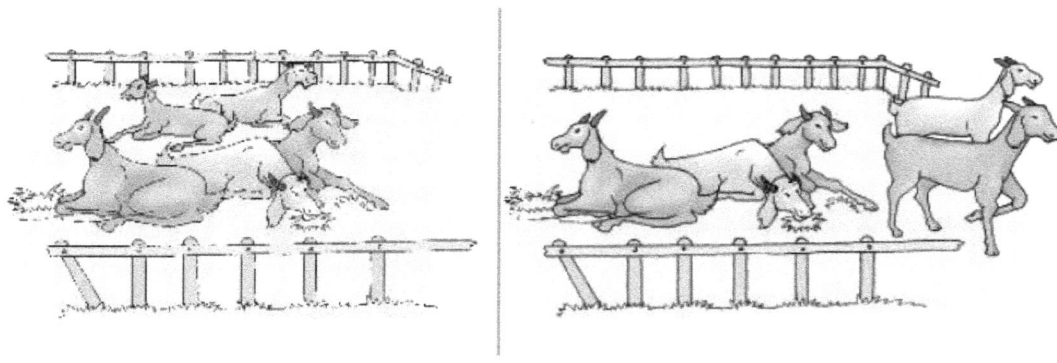

Answer:

Ramu is a little boy. He is very hard-working. He makes beautiful baskets out of wood splints. He has 5 pet animals in his farm. Two of them left for grazing in another farm. Thus, now the farm has only 3 pet animals left.

2. Complete the pattern.

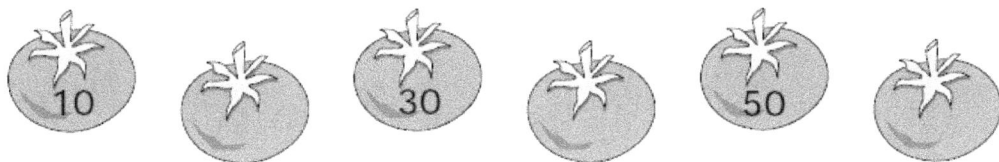

2   4   6   8

27   28   29

25   30   40

1   4   7

15   13   11

10   30   50

Answer:

2   4   6   8   10   12   14

27   28   29   30   31   32   33

25   30   35   40   45   50   55

1   4   7   10   13   16   19

15   13   11   9   7   5   3

10   20   30   40   50   60

3.

Count the shapes in the above picture.

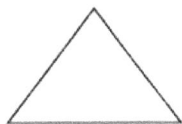  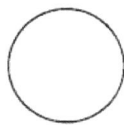 

Answer:

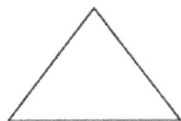  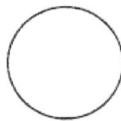 

Model Test Paper

1

Section I : Logical Reasoning

1. How many  are there in the box?

   (a) 22
   (b) 23
   (c) 19
   (d) 21

2. Complete the given number pattern.

   18 — ? — 20 — 21 — 22

   (a) 16   (b) 15
   (c) 17   (d) 19

3. Number of fishes swim to the left is

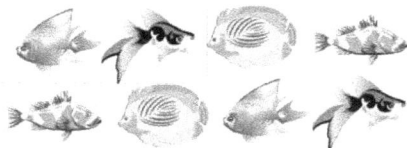

   (a) 2   (b) 3
   (c) 4   (d) 5

4. Minimum number of blocks a mouse run to reach the cake, if it moves only in horizontal and vertical direction, is

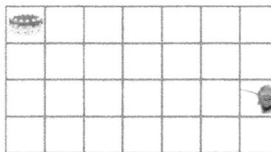

   = 1 BLOCK

   (a) 9   (b) 8
   (c) 10   (d) 7

5. Difference between the greatest and smallest number shown on the given butterfly is

   91, 87   19, 25
   27, 81   65, 13
   11   12

   (a) 87   (b) 81
   (c) 13   (d) 80

6. Which of the following shows counting by 5's?

   (a) 5 — 7 — 10 — 12 — 15

   (b) 3 — 7 — 10 — 15 — 20

   (c) 5 — 10 — 15 — 20 — 25

   (d) 5 — 10 — 12 — 15 — 18

7. The 7th gift box from the right end is

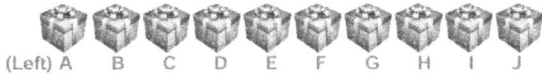

(Left) A   B   C   D   E   F   G   H   I   J

   (a) D   (b) C
   (c) E   (d) F

8. How many groups of 9 paper clips are there?

   (a) 9   (b) 27
   (c) 2   (d) 3

9. If 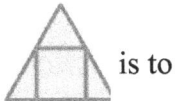 is to ⬛ , then

   ⬛ is to

   (a) ⬛   (b) ⬛

   (c) ⬛   (d) ⬛

10. There are _____ circles in the given figure.

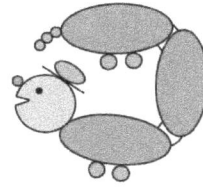

   (a) 14   (b) 10
   (c) 13   (d) 9

Section II : Mathematical Reasoning

11. Which number is correctly describing the subtraction shown below?

   (a) 9 − 4   (b) 10 − 4
   (c) 9 − 5   (d) 9 + 4

12. Which abacus shows the total number of balloons given here?

   (a) ⬛   (b) ⬛

   (c) ⬛   (d) ⬛

13. The difference between the number of stones in 6th column and 3rd column is

(a) 3   (b) 8

(c) 7   (d) 6

14. Number of Honey comb cells in the given figure is

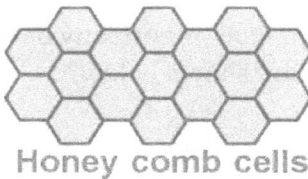

Honey comb cells

(a) 10 tens + 3 ones

(b) 10 tens + 2 ones

(c) 10 tens + 7 ones

(d) 10 tens + 5 ones

15. The given image is how many units tall?

1 unit

(a) 6 units   (b) 7 units

(c) 5 units   (d) 8 units

16. How many given letters are formed ONLY by curved lines?

A B C D E F G H I J K L M N O
P Q R S T U V W X Y Z

(a) 3   (b) 6

(c) 5   (d) 4

17. There are 8 legs. How many horses are there?

(a) 3   (b) 4

(c) 2   (d) 1

18. How many vertical lines are there in the given figure?

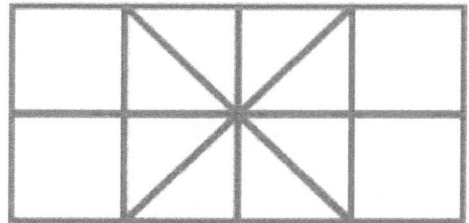

(a) 2   (b) 4

(c) 3   (d) 5

19. Kavita has fourteen strawberries. She eats five of them. Number sentence showing how many strawberries left with Kavita is_____.

(a) $14 - 5 = 9$ (b) $14 + 5 = 19$

(c) $14 - 5 = 8$ (d) $14 + 5 = 18$

20. A B C D E F G H I J K L M N O P Q R S T U V W X Y Z

The number of letters lying between which of the following options is the greatest?

(a) A and L   (b) C and M

(c) N and W   (d) Q and Z

21. Which of the following shows descending order?

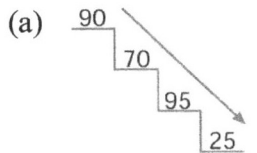

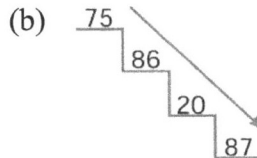

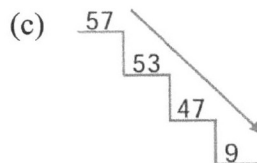

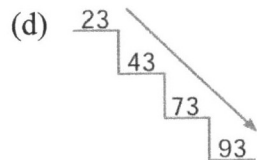

(a)
90
70
95
25

(b)
75
86
20
87

(c)
57
53
47
9

(d)
23
43
73
93

22. How much money is shown here?

(a) ₹ 70   (b) ₹ 75

(c) ₹ 76   (d) ₹ 71

23. The difference betwwen third and fifth balloon is

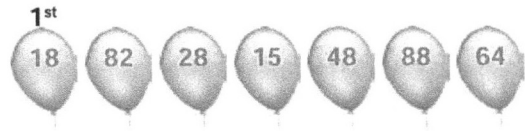

1ˢᵗ

18   82   28   15   48   88   64

(a) 18   (b) 30

(c) 20   (d) 23

24. I am less than 87 but greater than 85. What number am I?

85 < ? < 87

(a) 88   (b) 86

(c) 84   (d) 85

25. Which two numbers when added will give 2 tens – 8 ones?

(a) 4 + 3

(b) 4 + 8

(c) 2 + 2

(d) 2 + 4

Section III : Everyday Mathematics

26. Latika has 25 stickers. She gives 5 stickers to each of her student. Number of students who will get stickers is
   (a) 4   (b) 6
   (c) 3   (d) 5

27. Total length of Komal's and Beena's pencil is

   (a) 21 centimetres   (b) 31 centimetres
   (c) 17 centimetres   (d) 20 centimetres

28. Jiya picked 9 flowers. Ash picked two flowers. Mannu picked 5 flowers. How many flowers did the children pick in total?

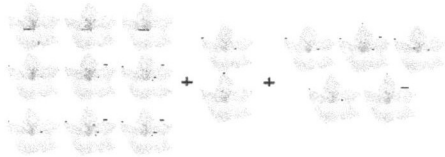

   (a) 16   (b) 14
   (c) 19   (d) 15

29. There are some dogs and cats in the playground. Total number of animals in the playground is

   (a) 16   (b) 19
   (c) 17   (d) 15

30. Out of 35 stamps, Anu gave 13 stamps to Neha. How many stamps does Anu have now?

   (a) 35   (b) 48
   (c) 22   (d) 21

31. A doll costs ₹ 19. Jenny has only ₹ 15 now. How much more money does she need to buy the doll?
   (a) ₹ 4   (b) ₹ 34
   (c) ₹ 3   (d) ₹ 5

32. The given poster of Apu shows different types of fishes. Which type of fish is least in number?

   (a)

   (b)

   (c)

   (d)

33. If there are 12 pears altogether and 5 are kept outside, then how many pears are there in the bag?

   (a) 8   (b) 6

   (c) 7   (d) 9

34. The total height of both the poles (A and B) together is

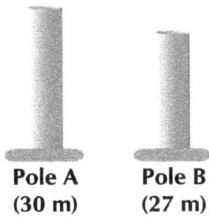

Pole A   **Pole B**
(30 m)   **(27 m)**

(a) 30 metres   (b) 57 metres

(c) 27 metres   (d) 67 metres

35. Which of the following T-shirts bears the number 3 tens + 3 ones?

(a)

(b)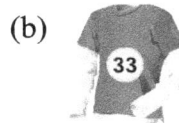

(c)

(d)

Model Test Paper

2

Section I : Logical Reasoning

1. How many different types of fruits are there in the basket?

   (a) 4   (b) 5
   (c) 7   (d) 6

2. If yesterday was Sunday , then tomorrow will be

Yesterday	Today	Tomorrow
Sunday	–	?

   (a) Monday   (b) Tuesday
   (c) Saturday   (d) Wednesday

3. Which smiley is 5th from the right end?

   (a) T   (b) R
   (c) Q   (d) U

4. Complete the given number pattern.

   (a) 22   (b) 24
   (c) 21   (d) 25

5. In the given image, the car is parked ———— the house.

   (a) Inside   (b) Outside
   (c) Above   (d) Below

6. Name the shape of the shaded face.

   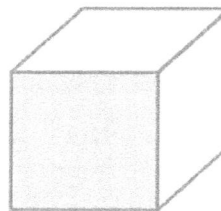

   (a) Circle   (b) Square
   (c) Oval   (d) Triangle

7. The given activity shows

   (a) Morning   (b) Afternoon
   (c) Evening   (d) Night

8. Select the figure which is as same as Figure (X).

Figure (X)

(a)

(b)

(c)

(d)

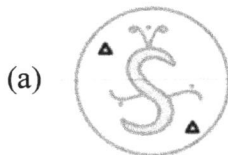

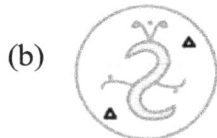

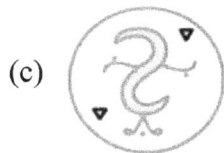

9. Which piece can be put together with shape P to make a square? Shape P

(a)

(b)

(c)

(d)

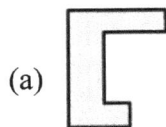

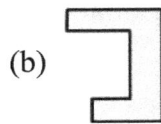

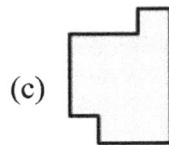

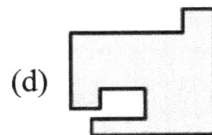

10. Rohit is taller than Samay but is shorter than Meeku. Who is the tallest?
   (a) Samay   (b) Meeku
   (c) Rohit   (d) None of these

Section II : Mathematical Reasoning

11. Which of the following options shows the largest number of pencils?

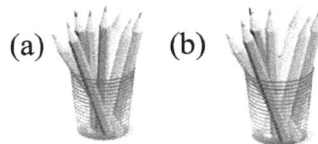

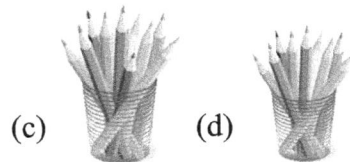

   (a)   (b)

   (c)   (d)

12. Which of the following subtraction is CORRECT?
   (a) $13 - 5 = 9$ (b) $19 - 4 = 15$
   (c) $17 - 7 = 12$ (d) $29 - 4 = 27$

13. If a rabbit starts jumping from 0, then it will finally reach at _____ in first Jump.

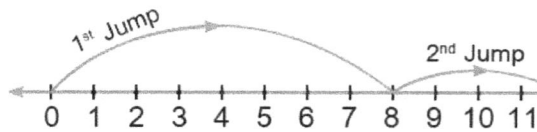

(a) $0 + 8 = 8$
(b) $8 - 4 = 4$
(c) $8 + 4 = 12$
(d) $12 + 8 = 20$

14. Which is the missing number in the number bond?

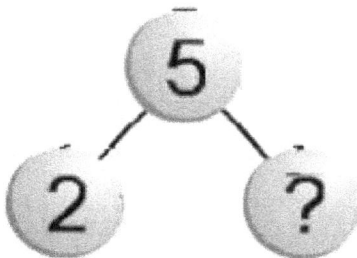

(a) 1
(b) 2
(c) 3
(d) 4

15. Elephant _____ is just before elephant A

(a) C
(b) E
(c) B
(d) D

16. The penguin is about _____ △ tall.

(a) 10
(b) 6
(c) 4
(d) 8

17. In which of the following options, numbers are arranged from the smallest to the greatest?
(a) 46, 25, 17, 3, 9   (b) 3, 9, 17, 25, 46
(c) 46, 25, 17, 9, 3   (d) 3, 9, 17, 46, 25

18. The number of straight lines in the given picture is

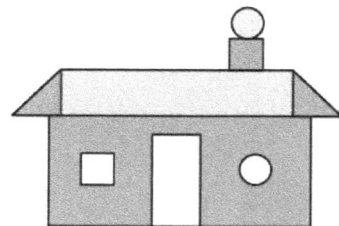

(a) 20
(b) 23
(c) 22
(d) 17

19. Find the number that is more than $5 + 6$ but less than $10 + 3$.
(a) 12
(b) 13
(c) 14
(d) 15

20. If ' ' means '−', then 8 3 = ?

(a) 4

(b) 5

(c) 0

(d) 3

Section III : Everyday Mathematics

21. Anjali had 18 apples . She put 3 apples into each bag . She used _____ bags.

(a) 8   (b) 6

(c) 9   (d) 5

22. How much amount of money is shown here?

(a) ₹ 40   (b) ₹ 70

(c) ₹ 60   (d) ₹ 50

23. Priya baked 6 cakes. She baked 3 more cakes than Beena. Beena baked _____ cakes.

(a) 2   (b) 4

(c) 3   (d) 6

24. Garima has 2 sticks A and B. Stick A is _____ units longer than stick B.

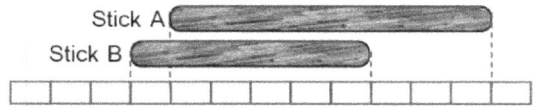

Each ☐ stands for 1 unit.

(a) 2   (b) 4

(c) 6   (d) 8

25. Anna had 17 balls. She gave away 6 balls. How many balls are left with her?

(a) 11   (b) 9

(c) 8   (d) 7

26. There are 12 horses. Three of them walk away. How many horses are left?

(a) 8

(b) 9

(c) 6

(d) 5

27. Mini has 14 toys and Riya has 5 toys. How many total toys both have?

(a) 15   (b) 19

(c) 9   (d) 20

28. Mohit needs to buy a chair and a lamp. How much does he need to pay?

Chair   Bear   Horse   Lamp   Duck

(a) ₹ 15   (b) ₹ 70

(c) ₹ 22   (d) ₹ 45

29. Sarah had 16 toffees. If she put all the toffees in 4 boxes equally, then she has _____ toffees in each box.

   (a) 2   (b) 4
   (c) 6   (d) 8

30. Out of 9 books that Ruchi has, 3 are Mathematics books and the rest are English books. Ruchi has _____ English books.
   (a) 4   (b) 7
   (c) 8   (d) 6

Section IV : Achievers Section

31. 2 tens 7 ones − 1 tens 6 ones = ?
   (a) 17   (b) 16
   (c) 11   (d) 19

32. There are _____ more birds than cats.

   (a) 3   (b) 8
   (c) 4   (d) 9

33. The number of squares is _____ more than the number of triangles.

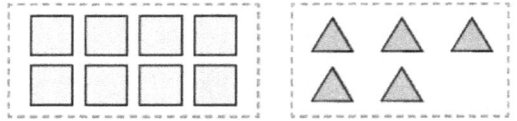

   (a) 3 tens − 0 ones
   (b) 2 tens
   (c) 5 ones − 2 ones
   (d) 8 ones + 2 ones

34. The missing number in the box is

$$
\begin{array}{r}
7\ 6 \\
-\ \square\ 4 \\
\hline
2\ 2 \\
\end{array}
$$

   (a) 5   (b) 4
   (c) 3   (d) 2

35. Which abacus shows 3 more than 61?

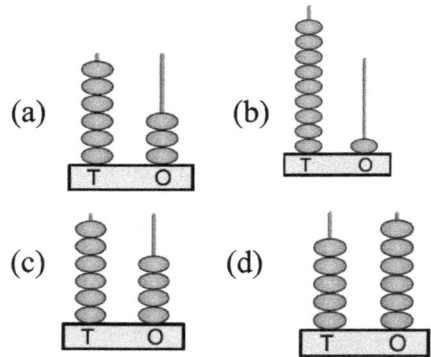

Answer Keys

Scan the QR Code to see the Hints and Solutions

Access Content Online on Dropbox: https://www.dropbox.com/scl/fi/x1il8nzpuzwm1qyz8yycu/NSO-01-Science-Olympiad-Hints-and-Solutions.pdf?rlkey=kzkx1753ie7dfs4rlkt3yo4pa&dl=0

SECTION 1: MATHEMATICAL REASONING

1. NUMBERS

Answer Key									
1. (c)	2. (d)	3. (b)	4. (c)	5. (d)	6. (a)	7. (b)	8. (b)	9. (c)	10. (a)
11. (b)	12. (b)	13. (d)	14. (b)	15. (a)	16. (a)	17. (b)	18. (c)	19. (c)	20. (c)

HOTS				
1. (c)	2. (b)	3. (d)	4. (c)	5. (a)

2. ADDITION

ANSWER KEY									
1. (a)	2. (b)	3. (d)	4. (b)	5. (b)	6. (a)	7. (d)	8. (b)	9. (a)	10. (c)
11. (b)	12. (c)	13. (b)	14. (b)	15. (b)	16. (d)	17. (b)	18. (c)	19. (c)	20. (d)

HOTS				
1. (b)	2. (c)	3. (c)	4. (c)	5. (a)

3. SUBTRACTION

ANSWER KEY									
1. (a)	2. (b)	3. (a)	4. (b)	5. (d)	6. (b)	7. (c)	8. (a)	9. (b)	10. (b)
11. (a)	12. (b)	13. (a)	14. (b)	15. (b)	16. (a)	17. (b)	18. (a)	19. (b)	20. (c)

HOTS

1. (a)	2. (a)	3. (a)	4. (b)	5. (b)	6. (b)	7. (d)	8. (c)	9. (b)	10. (b)

4. MEASUREMENT

Answer Key

1. (a)	2. (d)	3. (a)	4. (a)	5. (b)	6. (d)	7. (a)	8. (d)	9. (b)	10. (a)
11. (d)	12. (a)	13. (d)	14. (a)	15. (c)	16. (c)	17. (a)	18. (a)	19. (d)	20. (c)

HOTS

1. (d)	2. (a)	3. (b)	4. (d)	5. (b)

5. TIME

Answer Key

1. (a)	2. (c)	3. (b)	4. (a)	5. (b)	6. (c)	7. (d)	8. (c)	9. (d)	10. (b)
11. (a)	12. (a)	13. (d)	14. (d)	15. (a)	16. (a)	17. (c)	18. (a)	19. (b)	20. (c)

HOTS

1. (b)	2. (d)	3. (a)	4. (c)	5. (a)

6. MONEY

Answer Key

1. (c)	2. (d)	3. (c)	4. (d)	5. (a)	6. (b)	7. (b)	8. (c)	9. (a)	10. (b)
11. (b)	12. (b)	13. (a)	14. (d)	15. (b)	16. (c)	17. (c)	18. (b)	19. (a)	20. (a)

HOTS

1. (b)	2. (b)	3. (d)	4. (b)	5. (b)

7. GEOMETRICAL SHAPES

				Answer Key					
1. (b)	2. (c)	3. (c)	4. (a)	5. (b)	6. (d)	7. (b)	8. (a)	9. (b)	10. (a)
11. (b)	12. (c)	13. (d)	14. (c)	15. (b)	16. (b)	17. (b)	18. (c)	19. (b)	20. (d)

	HOTS			
1. (c)	2. (d)	3. (a)	4. (b)	5. (a)

SECTION 2: LOGICAL REASONING

1. PATTERNS

				Answer Key					
1. (a)	2. (b)	3. (b)	4. (c)	5. (b)	6. (d)	7. (b)	8. (c)	9. (b)	10. (d)
11. (a)	12. (d)	13. (b)	14. (b)	15. (c)	16. (d)	17. (b)	18. (c)	19. (b)	20. (a)

2. ODD ONE OUT

				Answer Key					
1. (d)	2. (d)	3. (c)	4. (c)	5. (d)	6. (b)	7. (a)	8. (d)	9. (b)	10. (b)
11. (d)	12. (c)	13. (d)	14. (a)	15. (d)	16. (c)	17. (c)	18. (b)	19. (a)	20. (d)

3. ANALOGY

				Answer Key					
1. (b)	2. (a)	3. (a)	4. (d)	5. (c)	6. (d)	7. (a)	8. (b)	9. (d)	10. (a)
11. (c)	12. (a)	13. (b)	14. (d)	15. (a)	16. (b)	17. (b)	18. (d)	19. (b)	20. (a)

4. RANKING TEST

Answer Key

1. (c)	2. (b)	3. (a)	4. (c)	5. (d)	6. (a)	7. (a)	8. (a)	9. (d)	10. (b)
11. (c)	12. (b)	13. (a)	14. (a)	15. (b)	16. (a)	17. (b)	18. (c)	19. (c)	20. (b)

5. PROBLEMS BASED ON FIGURES

Answer Key

1. (c)	2. (d)	3. (a)	4. (b)	5. (a)	6. (a)	7. (d)	8. (b)	9. (b)	10. (c)
11. (b)	12. (d)	13. (c)	14. (b)	15. (b)	16. (b)	17. (b)	18. (d)	19. (b)	20. (d)

MODEL TEST PAPER–1

Answer Key

1. (b)	2. (d)	3. (c)	4. (b)	5. (d)	6. (c)	7. (a)	8. (d)	9. (b)	10. (d)
11. (a)	12. (c)	13. (a)	14. (c)	15. (d)	16. (b)	17. (c)	18. (d)	19. (a)	20. (a)
21. (c)	22. (c)	23. (c)	24. (b)	25.(b)	26. (d)	27. (d)	28. (a)	29. (d)	30.(c)
31. (a)	32. (d)	33. (c)	34. (b)	35. (b)					

MODEL TEST PAPER–2

Answer Key

1. (b)	2.(b)	3. (b)	4. (a)	5. (b)	6. (b)	7. (a)	8. (b)	9. (c)	10. (b)
11. (c)	12. (b)	13. (a)	14. (c)	15. (b)	16. (d)	17. (b)	18. (d)	19. (a)	20. (b)
21. (b)	22. (c)	23. (c)	24. (a)	25. (a)	26. (b)	27. (b)	28. (d)	29. (b)	30. (d)
31. (c)	32. (a)	33. (c)	34. (a)	35. (c)					

Appendix

There are different organizations that conduct these examinations and covering all of them is not needed as the focus should be to understand the main type of exams conducted. They are similar for these organizations with the difference being the change in name of the exam.

Science Olympiad Foundation (SOF)		
S. No.	Name of Exam	Grade
1.	National Science Olympiad (NSO)	Class 1-10
2.	National Cyber Olympiad (NCO)	Class 1-10
3.	International Mathematics Olympiad (IMO)	Class 1-10
4.	International English Olympiad (IEO)	Class 1-10
5.	International Commerce Olympiad (ICO)	Class 1-10
6.	International General Knowledge Olympiad (IGKO)	Class 1-10
7.	International Social Studies Olympiad (ISSO)	Class 1-10
Indian Talent Olympiad (ITO)		
S. No.	Name of Exam	Grade
1.	International Science Olympiad (ISO)	Class 1-12
2.	International Math Olympiad (IMO)	Class 1-12
3.	English International Olympiad (EIO)	Class 1-12
4.	General Knowledge International Olympiad (GKIO)	Class 1-12
5.	International Computer Olympiad (ICO)	Class 1-12
6.	International Drawing Olympiad (IDO)	Class 1-12
7.	National Essay Olympiad (NESO)	Class 1-12
8.	National Social Studies Olympiad (NSSO)	Class 1-12
EduHeal Foundation		
S. No.	Name of Exam	Grade
1.	Eduheal International Cyber Olympiad (ICO)	Class 1-12
2.	Eduheal International English Olympiad (IEO)	Class 1-12
3.	National Interactive Math Olympiad (NIMO)	Class 1-12
4.	National Interactive Science Olympiad (NISO)	Class 1-12
5.	International General Knowledge Olympiad (IGO)	Class 1-12
6.	National Space Science Olympiad (NSSO)	Class 1-12

Humming Bird Education

S. No.	Name of Exam	Grade
1.	Humming Bird Commerce Competency Olympiad (HCC)	Class 1-12
2.	Humming Bird Cyber Olympiad (HCO)	Class 1-12
3.	Humming Bird English Olympiad (HEO)	Class 1-12
4.	Humming Bird General Knowledge Olympiad (HGO)	Class 1-12
5.	Humming Bird Hindi Olympiad (HHO)	Class 1-12
6.	Humming Bird Mathematics Olympiad (HMO)	Class 1-12
7.	Humming Bird Science Olympiad (HSO)	Class 1-12
8.	Humming Bird Aptitude and Reasoning Olympiad (ARO)	Class 1-12
9.	Humming Bird Spelling Competition (Spell BEE)	Class 1-12
10.	Humming Bird Language Olympiad	Class 1-12

International Assessments for Indian Schools (IAIS) (MacMillan and EEA Collaboration)

S. No.	Name of Exam	Grade
1.	IAIS Maths Olympiad	Class 3-12
2.	IAIS ScienceOlympiad	Class 3-12
3.	IAIS English Olympiad	Class 3-12
4.	IAIS Digital Technologies Olympiad	Class 3-12

SilverZone Foundation

S. No.	Name of Exam	Grade
1.	International Informatics Olympiad	Class 1-12
2.	International Olympiad of Mathematics	Class 1-12
3.	International Olympiad of Science	Class 1-12

Unified Council

S. No.	Name of Exam	Grade
1.	Unified Council Cyber Exam	Class 1-12
2.	Unified International English Olympiad.	Class 1-12
3.	Unified International Mathematics Olympiad (UIMO)	Class 1-12

Unicus

S. No.	Name of Exam	Grade
1.	Unicus Non-Routine Mathematics Olympiad (UNRMO)	Class 1-11
2.	Unicus Mathematics Olympiad (UMO)	Class 1-11

3.	Unicus Science Olympiad (USO)	Class 1-11
4.	Unicus English Olympiad (UEO)	Class 1-11
5.	Unicus Cyber Olympiad (UCO)	Class 1-11
6.	Unicus General knowledge Olympiad (UGKO)	Class 1-11
7.	Unicus Critical Thinking Olympiad (UCTO)	Class 1-11
CREST (Online Mode)		
S. No.	**Name of Exam**	**Grade**
1.	Mathematics (CMO)	Classes KG-10
2.	Science (CSO)	Classes KG-10
3.	English (CEO)	Classes KG-10
4.	Computer (CCO)	Classes 1-10
5.	Reasoning (CRO)	Classes 1-10
6.	Spell Bee Summer (CSB)	Classes 1-8
7.	Spell Bee Winter (CSBW)	Classes 1-8
8.	Mental Maths (MMO)	Classes 1-12
9.	Green Warrior Olympiad (GWO)	Classes 1-12

How To Apply?

Anyone willing to participate in the Olympiad exam can follow these steps to apply for the exam:

☞ Log in to the official website of the conducting organization.

☞ Find the Registration Option to register

☞ Fill up the details such as Student Name, Parent Name, School Name, Class, Postal Address, E-mail Address, Password, etc.

☞ Select the subjects you want to apply for. Pay the necessary registration fees and you are done.

☞ You will receive necessary details on your email id.

There are no minimum marks required by the Olympiad conducting organizations to apply for the exam.

Awards

Based on the organization rules, students as well as schools participating in these exams are awarded with several recognitions based on the marks they score.

🕐🕐🕐

www.ingramcontent.com/pod-product-compliance
Lightning Source LLC
Chambersburg PA
CBHW080520090426
42734CB00015B/3117